HOPE
Love's Greatest Gift

*Now hope does not disappoint, because the
love of God has been poured out in our hearts
by the Holy Spirit who was given to us.
Romans 5:5 (NKJV)*

Catherine Petersen Duran

Aventine Press

Back cover photo by Jenetta Lea Penner
(www.**jenettalea**.com)

Published by Aventine Press
1023 4th Ave #204
San Diego CA, 92101
www.aventinepress.com

ISBN: 1-59330-412-9

Printed in the United States of America

Endorsements

In knowing Catherine and seeing her deal with tragedy and loss in her life, three words come to mind – onward Christian soldier! Her strength and tenacity clearly come from the one in whom she places her hope and trust, Jesus and his word. If you feel like there's no hope and are struggling with grief and pain, this book is for you. It will encourage you and point you in the right direction for hope, healing, and wholeness. If you haven't had to travel down the grief path, this book can help a friend who has or it will better equip you should you take that journey someday.
- Mark Manion, motivational speaker, and author of "Unfinished Miles."

Captivating is the first word that came to mind as I began to read Catherine's book. My heart was drawn into her life experiences as she eloquently described her ups, downs and victories. Her story is so well integrated with God as central in her life, that it gave me courage and hope that I could naturally apply to my own circumstances. Catherine's style of writing is authentic, charismatic and emotionally impacting which draws the reader in immediately. I began to

read her manuscript and could not put it down. I would recommend this book to anyone who desires to be encouraged, refreshed and filled with hope in our powerful, healing God.
-Teresa Quinn, Pastor of Small Groups at Canyon View Christian Fellowship (www.cvcf.com)

If you are in the wake of love and loss then it is no accident that this book found its way to you. I am privileged to know Catherine Petersen Duran as a powerful, dynamic and talented worship leader who speaks and sings tenderly, openly and humorously to the truth she not only knows but lives so well.

When the unthinkable happened and her life was forever changed she turned to the One who changes not. You, dear reader are invited to come, taste and see that the Lord is good even in the midst of tragedy and loss. Catherine's faith, hope, and love produced a new song which is clearly heard in the pages of "Hope: Loves Greatest Gift" *as scripture after scripture brings a greater understanding of the healing power of God's word and the hope of joy coming in the mourning.*
-Lynda Miller, Pastor/Founder New Beginnings Counseling Services President, San Diego Evening Aglow

I have known Catherine Duran for many years now and have had the privilege to minister together with her at many retreats and conferences. Her life is a living testimony of the message of hope she shares. "Hope: Love's Greatest Gift" *is a page turner and will encourage you to have hope in whatever desperate situation you face in life.*

-Catherine Martin, Founder and President Quiet Time Ministries (www.quiettime.org)

Catherine Duran's courageous story of her path from pain and despair to hope and healing will inspire all those who have suffered great loss in their lives. Catherine shows how steadfast trust in God and the transforming power of God's can bring restoration to even the most wounded soul.

-Mark L. Strauss, PhD Professor of New Testament Bethel University, San Diego, California www.bethel.edu

Meet the Author

Catherine Petersen Duran is an accomplished singer, worship leader and speaker. For the past 20 years, she has dedicated her life to sharing God's message of hope and encouragement at numerous women's ministry events, conferences and retreats.

Catherine has a bachelor's degree in music from Vanguard University. She has audited classes at Fuller Theological Seminary, titled, "Small Groups," "Prayer," and one that made an especially lasting impact, "Women in Transition" with Professor Roberta Hestenes. Her worship leading began at Westminster Christian Assembly in Orange County, California where she served on staff as music director.

She received further worship training while attending New Life Church in Colorado Springs under the dynamic leadership of Associate Pastor, Ross Parsley. Catherine performed and sang back up with Don Moen, on Integrity's *Rivers of Joy*, assisted in the choral directing of *Lord of the Harvest*, and performed on New Life's *Shine Your Light Through the Window* worship and prayer album produced for AD2000 United Prayer Track with Dr. C. Peter Wagner, coordinator.

Catherine was on staff at the prominent worldwide ministry, Focus on the Family with Dr. James Dobson, in Colorado Springs where she served as guest relations assistant for four years. This position gave her many opportunities to share with, pray with, and encourage ministry guests.

Catherine currently serves as interim music director at Rancho Bernardo Baptist Church, and teaches private music lessons in her home studio. She recently returned from a mission trip to Cameroon, Africa where she spoke to a group of missionary women—an experience, she says, that was thrilling yet humbling.

As a member of NEWIM (Network of Evangelical Women in Ministry), and Christian Women Speakers, Catherine's life commitment is to encourage others in their walk of faith, whether new believers or long-time Christians. Her passion for missions and reaching the lost is contagious as she draws the attention to her Lord and Savior Jesus Christ through worship leading, singing, and speaking.

Acknowledgments

First of all, I owe a special thank you to my husband, Tony, for allowing me to spend hours and hours pouring over manuscripts without a single complaint. Your constant support and belief in me has given me the courage to put legs to my story. You are truly a gift from God!

A great big Italian hug for my sweet friend and brilliant editor, Summer Groenendal. Your heart for the Lord and ear for flow and continuity made this work sing. Thank you for pulling me through to completion.

The book cover is designed by Malane Newman. Thank you, Malane for encouraging me through the development of my website, which has launched me into more speaking events and sharing God's message of hope. Your incredible talent and creativity has given me wings!

Finally, and certainly not least, I want to thank my Lord and Savior, Jesus Christ. Without you, Lord, my story would have no purpose. Your design and orchestration of my life has brought me to the point of sharing it without apologies. You alone are the reason I sing and the only reason I am able to stand and share these words. You give me the strength and the desire to pour my heart and soul out for your purposes. Take this work as I lay it at your altar. I present this message of Hope to you as an offering of my love. Please use it for your glory!

Dedication

I dedicate this book to my wonderful children: Nathan, Krista, Erin Joy, James and Toni Nicole, and to all my friends and family members who have walked through difficulties of their own. There are too many to list, but you know who you are.

May this book be a reminder of my love and respect for you, and a public recognition of your faith and courage through tough times. Together, we will fight this fight of faith and will stand victorious, because the power of Jesus Christ works in us. Never ever forget, there is always hope!

Table of Contents

Introduction

Life is an obstacle course. Walking along life's path, sometimes the road is straight and level. Sometimes you'll climb a hill or two. Then, somewhere along the way, you'll most likely encounter a wall blocking your path. It's enough to interrupt your pace and catch you off guard. The obstacle can prove challenging, but with some grit and effort you manage to scale the wall and walk on. Then there are the mud pits.

A mud pit would be anything that slows you down and causes you to be discouraged and eventually give up. If you fall into one and stay there long enough, it could ultimately destroy you. The pit represents grief that could be caused by the loss of a loved one—through death or divorce—or it could be that you or one of your family members has been struck with a serious illness. Whatever it is, it causes you to feel trapped, like there's no hope for survival.

Difficult times can bring out the worst in us. Our feelings of anger, frustration, and sorrow seem to ooze out, uncontrollably, from deep within our soul. This is similar to a physical wound that festers and bleeds. It's not pretty. But only one thing is certain. Whether it's self-induced or outside of our control, the mud pit will surely get our attention.

Unfortunately, there is no shortcut through the painfully annoying muck. As dismaying as this may seem, you *do* have a choice. When you find yourself kicking and flailing in the pits of life, you can decide to pitch a tent on the "why?" question, or you can ask, "now what?" and examine the choices you have when you are blinded by the pain. You can either remain in a hopeless and overwhelming mud pit, alone and in despair, or you can accept a hand up and get out.

In this book, I tell my story how as a young woman blindsided by tragedy, I was delivered and healed through my deep-rooted faith in God. My faith was established by hearing God's word. Not just reading it, but also hearing it with spiritual understanding. God's word is filled with promises and provisions for all who are members of his family. Our job, as his children, is to believe God and trust his word as the ultimate source of truth for our lives.

Isaiah 43:2 is a perfect example of God's assurance to us as his children.

> *When you pass through the waters,*
> *I will be with you; and when you pass*
> *through the rivers; they will not sweep*
> *over you. When you walk through the*
> *fire, you will not be burned; the flames*
> *will not set you ablaze.*

I promise you, I'm an ordinary person, but I found extraordinary strength to make it out of one of the most depressing mud pits in my life. My key to victory was based on the truth of God's Holy Word.

A key that is available to everyone who chooses to use it.

Should you choose to grasp it, this key will open a whole universe of understanding, and a lifetime of hope and healing. Its message is timeless, crossing cultural lines and any religious boundaries because it is based on the pure, infallible, Word of God.

Chapter One:
Love Demands Sacrifice

"Love bears all things, believes all things,
hopes all things, endures all things."
1 Corinthians 13:7

Carefully placing one foot in front of the other, I made my way to the front of the large classroom. My hands were clammy and my knees wobbled, but I kept moving. For weeks I drilled the passage into my mind, phrase after phrase, line by line, until I could practically recite it in my sleep.

There I stood, a short, shy, scrawny girl. I was nothing special to look at. The other kids teased me mercilessly, calling me names like pipsqueak and shrimp. Constantly feeling like a failure, I wrestled with feelings of inadequacy to the point of being physically sick at times.

Somehow, at that moment it didn't matter that I was scared to death. Being shy wasn't even enough to stop me. I was driven. I was only ten years old and about to stand in front of a crowd of adults and peers to recite the entire 23rd chapter of the book of Psalm, but there seemed to be a stronger force behind me that was driving me towards the challenge. It was sheer determination and God's strength that pushed me beyond fear to a place I had never been before.

That year, the tide had begun to slowly turn and my self-esteem began to improve. The more I read and studied the Bible the stronger I felt inside. The voice of God echoed through His written word, replacing my fears and canceling the unspoken lies that I was of no value. My child-faith simply grabbed hold of what I studied, and like a pit bull, I held on tenaciously to what I learned. Even though I was young, I knew enough to stand firmly in the face of self-doubt.

Finally, I landed at the front of the room, turned and faced the crowd. The sea of faces before me sent me into an emotional tailspin. Gripped by fear, I could only stare at my feet. After what seemed like an eternity, I quickly whispered a prayer, "Dear God...please help me."

I took one deep breath, lifted my head and began. *"The Lord is my shepherd. I shall not want."* My voice cracked and sounded feeble at first, but with each phrase, I gained momentum. I continued.

> *He maketh me lie down in green pastures: he leadeth me beside the still waters. He restores my soul: he leadeth me in the paths of righteousness for his name's sake. Yea, though I walk through the valley of the shadow of death, I will fear no evil: for thou art with me; thy rod and thy staff they comfort me. Thou preparest a table before me in the*

presence of mine enemies: thou anointest my head with oil; my cup runneth over. Surely goodness and mercy shall follow me all the days of my life: and I will dwell in the house of the Lord forever. (Psalm 23 KJV)

As the last line spilled out, a smile of relief erupted on my face. *I did it!*

20 years later in Irvine, California

Erin Joy, now three months old, was hungry and tired. I was just tired. My body sank into the over-stuffed recliner in our family room. As a mother of three, the routine was second nature to me. Propping my feet up, I welcomed the chance to sit and relax while nursing my youngest child. I thought back to my seventh month of pregnancy when I was diagnosed with pre-labor and was ordered to bed rest.

I was a little, young pregnant woman carrying about 60 pounds of baby weight wobbling around the house, with feet and hands swelling almost beyond recognition in addition to the continual flu-like symptoms! I was like a 175 pound, PMS-ridden, morning-sick, pre-menopausal-young mom who was tired, sick, frustrated, uncomfortable, and extremely restless! I didn't know what to do with myself.

The doctor said the combination of the rest and medication would slow down the contractions. The medication did the trick, but it left me feeling shaky and bloated.

The hours and days leading up to my labor seemed to pass in slow motion, accentuated by my state of absolute boredom. My condition prevented me from cooking dinner, washing a load of clothes, pushing my kids on the swing outside, or even going to church. At first I thought I would be able to catch up on some reading, but quickly dropped that idea. As another side effect of the medication, I had blurred vision.

We had plans to move from San Diego to Orange County as soon as the baby was born. Rick had been installed as Senior Pastor of a small church and we were anxious to get moved and begin our new position. But every time I got up to pack a box, the contractions would get stronger. My body was sending me a clear message: *you'll be very sorry later if you don't lie down and put your feet up!*

I wondered how I was going to be able to pack an entire household while lying flat on my back. Slowly, one box at a time and resting in between, putting my feet up as often as possible, I made progress. The grueling ordeal stretched out for nearly three months.

The experience morphed from frustrating to humiliating. Before, I had always taken pride in my neat and tidy home. My kids were always well dressed and groomed and dinner was prepared and ready to eat the moment my husband's foot stepped in the front door. Now I was trapped in my weakened state and could barely make the kids' breakfast before the onset of contractions.

I felt like I was competing in a contest to see how quickly I could finish a task before the pain forced me down. At lunchtime, we had a re-match. My opponent was the clock. It was a test of speed that drained every speck of energy I had left. Simple routines were overwhelming.

I am eternally thankful for the dear friends and family who rescued us. I couldn't have told you which box the toaster was in, but the entire house got packed up just in time. One week after Erin Joy was born we said goodbye to our home, neighborhood, and church family.

Three months later we were settled into our new position and our new life. Our home, once again, was filled with the harmonious sounds of children playing. Our 5-year-old Krista could entertain herself for hours. Her short blonde pigtails and begging-to-be-pinched rosy cheeks captured anyone's heart. She loved to play house and often role-played with her brother, or any willing soul, for that matter. One day, it was with her friend, Andy.

"I'll be the mommy, and you be the daddy, 'kay?" she would chirp, with her contagious smile. "How about I make us some dinner? You hungry?" Her voice sang the question.

But what really tugged on your heartstrings was when she sang cheerfully in the mornings, "Jesus loves me, this I know. For the Bible tells me so…"

Our firstborn, 7-year-old Nathan, was smart as a whip. We knew he was different from most kids when his preschool teacher reported, "Nathan can read all the months of the year from the calendar and can spell the days of the week."

I was even more amazed to discover that he recognized the name of every student in the class.

Frequently, his wit caught us off guard. One time, when we were tucking Nathan and Krista into bed, Rick turned down the comforter to reveal the name *KRISTA* boldly written on the bottom sheet with black, permanent marker. Rick and I eyed each other, reading each other's minds. We knew that Krista hadn't learned to write letters yet and this printing job was darn near textbook perfect. We were certain of the culprit.

"Who did this?" Rick asked, directing his gaze at our son. Nathan shrugged and casually pointing to his sister answered, "It's *her* name, why don't you ask *her*?"

Erin Joy was falling asleep. I leaned my head back on the cushion, gazing outside. It was another beautiful day. The bright blue sky was the perfect backdrop to the sun's rays bursting through the branches of the tree just outside the patio door. I closed my eyes, relishing the fleeting moment.

On this particular morning we had two houseguests, Joey, 18 months and 3-year-old Andy. Our friends, Dave and Debbie Lurker were on vacation in Hawaii. I figured that if I took care of their boys this week, when Rick and I took *our* Hawaii trip they would watch our three kids. I was truly happy for them, but right now all I wanted was to be our little family again.

Putting my own feelings aside, I talked myself through it and I realized that it wasn't going to be all that bad. Over the past several years of motherhood, I developed the fine art of multi-tasking. I kept my normal daily schedule, doubled my dinner recipes, and started the bath and bedtime routine an hour earlier. Still, let's face it, five children under the age of seven in the best of circumstances is a houseful!

Rick called that afternoon. "How are *you* doing, Babe?" he asked. Hearing my tired voice, he assured me he would be home early and that he would give me some time off. We hung up but not before exchanging our usual "I love you." I clung to his hope-filled words as fuel for the next four hours of housework and tending to children.

Sure enough, at two o'clock right on the dot, Rick breezed through the back door greeting me with a broad smile. He reached down and cupped Erin's head in his hand, bending down to place a careful kiss on her forehead.

"How's Daddy's little angel?" He whispered. "Look at these tiny little fingers. Look how relaxed she is. Like a little rag doll. What does she have to worry about? That's it my sweet Erin Joy. You just go ahead and sleep. Everything's OK."

He looked up at me with pride and a twinkle in his eyes. There's no hiding that kind of pride and Rick certainly didn't try. Slowly and deliberately he knelt beside the recliner, shifted his body and leaned towards me to place a gentle kiss on my lips. His kisses still triggered those romantic flutters that made my heart skip a beat, even after nearly ten years of marriage. I welcomed the pleasant surprise of affection. Exhausted, yet content, I returned his gaze, smiled and sighed, letting my head fall on his shoulder. He slid his arm around Erin and me and held us in a cozy embrace.

"You're such a good daddy," I whispered.

Rick took care to spend time alone with each child. He implemented this plan a few years earlier when Krista was just a toddler, because he wanted them to have a one-on-one time with Dad on a regular basis. This was a very big deal in our home and with each "date" the anticipation grew. Sometimes it would be lunch at McDonalds, another time it was a trip to the beach to build a sand castle fort. But every time, whether 30 minutes or two hours, it was worth the wait. They came home bubbling with excitement, eager to tell me all the details. Oh how they loved their "just me and Daddy date!"

That day, Nathan was due home from school in a couple hours, Joey was taking a nap, and Andy and Krista were playing upstairs. Since Erin Joy was fed, content and sleeping, Rick and I spent some time together on the family room sofa. This was one of those rare and treasured moments in which we found ourselves alone, and the home front relatively calm. So we talked.

"Have I told you today how beautiful you are?" Rick began. I knew he was priming me for something. There I was, still carrying extra baby fat, wearing my oldest, most comfortable, sweat outfit complete with baby spit up stains and no makeup. And my hair had been sadly neglected.

"What's up? Come on... tell me," I asked.

His friend and colleague Dwight Westover was speaking in Bakersfield the next day on the topic of Ministry on College Campuses. Dwight invited Rick to come along for support, especially since Rick had personal experience from starting a campus ministry at San Diego State University.

Dwight served the denomination headquarters as District Director of Youth Ministries. His job was overseer and supervisor of all youth ministers in the Southern California area. Since Rick worked as Youth Pastor eight of his ten years in ministry, he and Dwight knew each other well. Most of their careers they were separated by some distance, Dwight's office in Orange County and Rick's in San Diego. Now for the first time in years, they could meet for lunch, brainstorm together about ministry stuff and just hang out. Since we had moved to Irvine, they were just minutes apart.

Rick revealed their plan to fly to the conference in a rented plane later that night. He rationalized that if they flew out early in the morning, they would probably meet rainy weather and risk being late, but if they flew out that night and stayed in a hotel they would be well rested and not as crunched for time getting to the breakfast.

"I just think it makes more sense to go tonight rather than having to get up at the crack of dawn in the morning," he defended, sensing my hesitation.

All of this made a convincing case I had to admit. What I didn't know was that Rick and Dwight had been talking about "going flying" for weeks, but it never worked out. Rick was intrigued with small planes and couldn't resist the chance to explore a cockpit up close.

"If we leave tonight after the kids are in bed, then you only have half the day tomorrow alone—and I'll be back by dinner time."

He was always good at making a convincing argument. Sometimes I thought He should have been a lawyer instead of a pastor. The only thing holding him back was my look of distress. I could see him studying my eyes for a glimmer of support. He knew that I had spent the last four days with five children and still had not slept well since before Erin was born.

In return, I studied *his* eyes and watched his face as he struggled with the decision. He must have thought to himself, *do I follow the passion for my work and embrace the thrill of a small plane ride, or do I embrace my fatherly and husband responsibilities and stay home?*

Meanwhile, I tossed it over in my mind and tried to figure out how my husband could have the best of both worlds. Our love had stood many tests before. It seemed to me that this was yet another test.

"Dwight has been checking the weather conditions and wouldn't fly unless it was safe," he interrupted my thoughts.

At that instant, it struck me—Dwight was the pilot. Somewhere amidst moving, adjusting to the new pastoral position, dirty diapers and feedings, I vaguely remember Rick telling me that Dwight recently finished his training and was now a bona fide pilot. For some reason, this piece of information was unsettling and I could feel my stomach tighten.

I wrestled quietly, arguing with myself. *What kind of wife are you if you're only happy when he's at home with you? He has a ministry and God's plans can't get accomplished if he's wife-sitting. Maybe you should try being supportive and quit being so selfish.*

The pot of conflict in my heart and mind was boiling over.

Many wives stay home with the kids while hubby is gone on business trips. When he comes home, he'll probably bring me a little present, a token of his love and affection. Then I'll feel really guilty for feeling this way. It's just a few hours. I really shouldn't make a big deal out of this!

My trust for Rick's good judgment won over my concerns that afternoon, so I gave him my blessing to go, stuffing my reservations. How could I say no to him? He would go with or without my blessing, but of course, he was smart enough to ask for it, and I appreciated that.

"I'll be back tomorrow afternoon," he said with a smile, "and then you and I are going out. I already have a babysitter lined up. It'll be just the two of us."

The Lurkers were going to be there soon to pick up their boys. I tried to convince myself that things would settle down, my emotions would level off, and that I wouldn't feel so abandoned.

Rick knew me well and accurately read my struggle. About an hour later he suggested an idea to help make things easier for me. He knew I didn't like the fact that I'd be alone in a new neighborhood in a big house with three small kids. As I listened, I heard his effort to smooth the way for me and it was rather creative. He invited Dwight's wife, Ruth, to stay with me. That's right, he organized an old fashioned slumber party. I felt a little silly, yet strangely relieved.

As if on cue, at four o'clock that afternoon he took the baby from me and said, "Okay, go. Take off for a couple of hours. Go get something to eat, or go shopping or whatever *you* want. Just take a break from this house for a while. I'll take care of the kids. When you get back, we'll get ready for Bible study at church. After that, I'll tuck the kids in bed and then leave for Bakersfield. I'll be back before you can miss me."

I felt like a bird being let out of a cage. The knot in my stomach was melting away. I was so happy to be free, even though it was only for a short time.

Rick and I took a little extra time together before saying goodbye. It was good to feel his arms around me. Laying my head on his chest, I pressed my body into his. This was home. Right there in his arms was my safe place. I breathed deeply and gave him an extra squeeze.

I spent the next two hours alone with my thoughts. Well, God was there too, of course. We tossed a few ideas around over a fast food dinner.

After spending years reading God's word and hours in meditation and prayer, I had developed an intimate relationship with God through his Holy Spirit. The Bible calls him the "teacher, guide, and comforter." When I spend time alone meditating on what God's word says and what I know to be true of my life and ministry, the voice of God guides my thoughts.

As I happily chewed on my french fries, I entered into a dialogue with God.

You love your role as a wife and mother. True. But I was truly worn to the bone and didn't have the heart to tell my husband I needed him more than those pastors in Bakersfield did.

You are very proud of him. Yes, I am proud of him. Look at all he has accomplished. This past year he turned 33 years old and became the senior pastor of a small church in a growing middle-class community in the heart of Orange County. It was our ministry dream, come true!

You've grown up with this man. We were just kids when we got married—he was 23 and I was 21. Now, 10 years later, our house was filled with the sounds of a growing, healthy family and our days with ministry and service to God.

For us, ministry had always been a way of life and our home always had an open door. When preparing dinner, I could never be exactly sure how many mouths I'd be feeding. An unexpected visitor could drop by at any time. It was so common for young college students to hang around Rick, listening to his every word. They'd go to the gas station with him and run other errands with him just to spend more time listening to his thoughts and ideas on church planting or discipleship. And if they were around at dinnertime, naturally, I'd just set another plate.

Must I share him so much? Couldn't he be more ordinary? Why can't he just be content to stay home and prepare sermons for Sunday? Let other ministers travel and speak and inspire the students. Does it have to be my husband?

The more I questioned, a picture formed in my mind. It was blurry at first but soon took shape. God had given me a wonderful, passionate man. He was a loving husband and caring father committed to meeting the needs of his family. Yet, God has also chosen him to be a bold young preacher that stirs hearts and lights flames under stuffy old church traditions. As hard as it was to share him and accept the man of God developing in him, I knew I wouldn't be happy with anything less.

The tender voice of God sliced through my thoughts. *"I am your Shepherd, remember? I am Rick's Shepherd also. You surrendered your life to me many years ago."*

The words of the familiar 23rd Psalm flashed in my mind. *The Lord is my Shepherd, I shall not want. He makes me lie down in green pastures, he restores my soul...*

A sweet assurance filled my heart as if the Lord said, *"Now, you must trust me, My child. I know you; I know Rick. And I gave you to each other knowing that you both need someone to love and cherish and support through this life of service to me. I am Your Shepherd and I will always lead you, even when it's hard. You must do your job and I'll do mine."*

Feeling convicted and ashamed, I prayed out loud when I got back into my car, "Oh, God, please forgive me. I'm feeling sorry for myself and totally selfish. Help me to be the wife he needs me to be. And to be the wife that you have prepared me to be. Give me the strength that I need to stay along side him. Sometimes I feel as if I'm running to keep up with him. I need you to show me, teach me, somehow make up for what I'm lacking. My heart desires to trust you more. Help me surrender to your way, and let go of mine."

That night after Bible study, Rick tucked the kids in bed one by one, just as he promised. From my seat downstairs, I could hear the giggles as he tickled and played with the two oldest. Then his deep warm voice softened as He prompted them through their prayers, first with Nathan, and then Krista. The cherished nightly ritual continued as he took the time to kiss and hug each one.

Turning towards the door, Rick called back over his shoulder, "Good night! I love you!"

The high-pitched squeaky voices bounced back as he closed the door, careful to leave it open just a crack.

"Night, Daddy. Love you too!"

He came down the stairs, bag in hand and a bounce in his step. I had to catch a moving target for one last kiss goodbye. There was a familiar sparkle in his deep brown eyes. He paused long enough to hold my face in his hands as he placed a kiss on my lips. "Thank you Hon. Thank you for letting me go. And, don't worry. I'll be home before you know it!" His lips brushed mine once more.

It was clear to me that just the thought of the trip was a thrill for him. As I watched him gather his things I heard myself call out to him, "Have a good time. I know you will!"

Closing the door behind him, I savored the sweetness of his goodbye. I had no reason to suspect that this brief ministry trip would set in motion a series of events that would change my life forever.

Chapter Two:
Flying by Faith

When troubles come my heart will say,
"Take flight my soul, on wings of faith."

When Dwight's wife Ruth and her 2-year-old daughter Michelle arrived, we brought their bags upstairs and got them settled. Then, Ruth blurted out a question that took me back about 10 years.

"Tell me, how did you and Rick meet?"

"Alright," I said, positioning myself on the edge of the bed, "this could take a while. Just stop me when you've had enough."

Right out of high school, I enrolled in Southern California College, a private Christian college. I brought every penny I had saved, plus a music scholarship, and naively entered the world of college life. My eyes were wide with anticipation to experience everything college life had to offer, including plenty of social activities.

We had ballgames, concerts, Bible studies, small get-togethers, and dorm parties for every occasion.

Most of the young men and women on campus took every opportunity to date. And while it was common for some girls to attend college only for the purpose of hunting for a husband, I didn't know of any healthy college girl who didn't have the slightest bit of hope that she might just meet her prince charming at school.

Personally, I wasn't sure what God's master plan was for my life, so I tried to stay open to avenues of ministry and enjoyed exploring future options of all kinds - including marriage. My obligations at work, school, music rehearsals, voice and piano practice, kept me running and left little time for dating, so I had to be creative.

Most of the guys I dated were those I knew from classes or from one of my singing groups. For the first two years of school, my dating consisted of friendly, informal get-togethers. We would go out to eat, go to a concert, shopping or walking the boardwalk at the beach.

Perhaps this is when my reputation as a hard-to-pin-down-girl began to develop. That's what the rumors said, anyway. But in my defense, there just wasn't anyone who swept me off my feet. Why would I commit to just *one* guy? Even the ones that got pretty serious didn't last very long.

Then one evening in the fall of my junior year, along with the turning of the leaves, came a change in my personal life. My friend Pat was singing in a concert at a local church and urged me to come. The "New Life Singers" were auditioning for new talent and Pat was intent on getting me in the group so we could travel and sing together.

"I really think you'll like our style. You'd fit right in—I just know it. At least come and listen for yourself."

Her bait was luring me.

"And I want you to meet Rick, the new guy in the group. Please?"

It sounded like a lot of fun, but I wasn't sure about trying out for a different group. *"But then again,"* I thought, *"maybe this group has better leadership and more opportunities. I'm a Music Major after all, so being in a more advanced group was probably a good career move."*

I didn't tell Pat what I was thinking but I agreed to go.

Pat had it all planned out. I would go and fall in love either with the group or the new guy—or both, and make the audition, right on the spot. The rest would be history.

When I arrived, I found some friends to sit with and quickly spied the attractive group stepping onto the platform after their name was announced. The place was packed, but I had a seat front and center so I could size up the group and the cute new Baritone.

From the very first song, they captured my attention. They sang with precision and style and their musicianship was impeccable. But their clearly expressed love for the Lord caught my attention the most. Each member of the group reflected a bold love for God. I witnessed their passion and deep faith as they sang and shared from their hearts. I was impressed and inspired.

And that baritone! When he stepped up to the microphone for his solo, out came this deep velvety voice that melted my heart.

"After the concert, I discretely asked Pat, "Is *he* dating anyone?"

"Nope," she said with a wink.

Before I could answer, Rick Petersen himself walked up to us, and cordially introduced himself to me. We looked at each other and smiled politely. He then invited us to grab a bite to eat with a group of his friends. The group director didn't allow for auditions that night, but I continued to explore the possibility in my mind.

Inside the restaurant, there were no seats left close to Rick, but I was content with the view from my seat. I was able to watch him from the other end of the long table without being obvious. He was confident and carried himself with a sense of purpose beyond his years. I noticed he was nearly always the focus of attention. Not because he demanded it, but because everyone else wanted to listen to Rick. He had a quick sense of humor, which kept everyone entertained, and he was in tune to the group like no one I had ever known. To the quiet one, he would draw them out. To the boisterous one, he would settle them down.

Everyone seemed to feel comfortable around him, including me, which was surprising. I hated to admit that he had stirred up some of my old insecurities. I had a difficult time believing that someone so smart and talented would be interested in me. After all, I was just a shy, scrawny girl who had to work her tail off to get B's. And Rick? Well, from what I gathered, he was a confident, well-spoken, straight-A student who was unbelievably gifted, and made friends easily.

Forget about it, Catherine, I thought, *you're out of his league.*

In the days after the concert, I felt as if there was a magnetic force drawing me to him. Almost everywhere I went, there he was. I went to eat in the school cafeteria and he would be there, greeting me with a warm smile. I wasn't completely sure if it qualified as flirting. It wasn't the words per se, but how he presented himself that infected me.

At that time, I worked as receptionist in the front office of the college. And guess who just happened to pop into the office, walking right by my desk on numerous occasions. It was Rick.

"Hello. I remember you from the concert. How are you today?" He asked in his deep warm voice.

He came by on more than one occasion after that, and always managing to say something charming. It never failed!

"Is the mail in yet?" Rick would ask, smiling, sometimes quite obviously flirting and other times more subtly. When he walked away, I'd want to check my pulse to see how fast my heart was racing.

By then, I'd had enough experience with guys to know when one was flirting with me. I suspected Rick was more than mildly interested. I tried to maintain my calm composure every time I saw him, but my stomach was doing flip-flops and I hated that my face turned red, betraying my true feelings. There was no escaping him, even if I wanted to.

Finally, after several weeks of these chance encounters he managed to ask me out. "Do you have anything going on Friday night?" he asked. "Would you like to go out after dinner, maybe for some dessert?"

This was the moment I'd secretly hoped for. There was just one problem. "Friday night I have rehearsal," I stammered. "The group I travel with has a rehearsal Friday night."

Rick thought for a minute and then with a twinkle in his eyes said, "Well, if you'd like, we could go later on after the rehearsal."

Smiling, I raised my eyebrows in surprise. I was impressed with his persistence. We agreed to meet in the dorm lobby at 7:45 p.m.

All during the rehearsal, I tried to stay calm but curiosity and intrigue had me on a hook. I was being reeled in. As the rehearsal dragged on, I began to feel torn by my commitment to the group and the desire to go out with Rick. At 8:00 p.m., I wrestled with wanting to leave early or staying on and possibly jeopardizing my chance to go out with Rick.

By 8:30 p.m. Rick surprised me by slipping in the back of the auditorium, looking handsome dressed in a black leather jacket. My heart sank as I thought, *He's probably getting tired of waiting, and this rehearsal isn't over yet. He probably wants to take a rain check.*

I excused myself for a moment and went back to explain. He seemed a bit disappointed, although understanding. Much to my delight, he didn't want to cancel. We agreed to stay with the original plan to go out, regardless of how late it was.

The minute the director began his final word of dismissal I sprinted to the dorms, being careful to walk slowly through the doors as I caught my breath.

"I was afraid that my hope would never become a reality," he said flashing me a warm smile. He then quickly escorted me to his car and opened the passenger door of his TR 4 for me to climb into. The whole time I was thinking, *Ok, be cool... don't blow this one. He seems too good to be true.*

He took me to a quaint little restaurant in Laguna called, The Cottage. We ate our pie and ice cream, completely engrossed in conversation. As the clock ticked on I listened to his stories about his family, where he came from and how he became a Christian. I found out what brought him to Southern California and especially SCC. Then he listened to all the same information about me. We both seemed to be listening with our hearts, because by the end of the evening, it was obvious that we had fallen for each other. And we fell hard!

Two hours later, even though it was late he drove us to the beach. The night was cool but still comfortable as we strolled down the sandy walkway towards the ocean. Our conversation flowed effortlessly as we watched the waves pounding against the shore. We both knew it was getting close to dorm curfew, but time didn't matter.

Casually, I stepped up on a large rock nearby which made me several inches taller. When I turned around to face him, we were conveniently eye to eye. It couldn't have been more perfect. The moon's rays glistened on the ocean, the stars shone brightly in the clear night sky.

Rick's eyes searched mine as if asking me if I was feeling what he was feeling. My heart was beating with nervous anticipation. Our hands touched first, and then he released his grip and carefully slid his arm around my waist as he drew closer. My heart pounded faster.

I think he wants to kiss me. Should I let him? My thoughts raced.

There wasn't much time to argue. The setting was too compelling and the chemistry too powerful. He couldn't resist the tug in his heart and I felt too safe and comfortable to stop him.

He leaned in without asking permission. With one hand cupping my face, he placed a soft and perfect kiss on my lips that lingered far beyond that night. It was one of those kisses that all the others are compared to.

Ruth was intrigued with our love story, but I could see that she was beginning to fade, so we agreed to finish the story in the morning. Besides, Ruth was in the early stages of pregnancy and I was anticipating at least one early morning feeding with Erin, so heading for bed was the smart thing to do.

After checking my three little ones, I fell exhausted into bed with thoughts of our budding romance still swimming in my head. I turned out the light, breathed a sigh and let the memory fade into the darkness.

All is well, I thought. *Soon I'll be rested and have more energy.*

"Lord thank you for this day," I prayed. "Thank you for bringing me some "big" people company. Now, I have a very special request. I need to sleep. I mean *really* sleep. Could you help Erin sleep four or five hours straight tonight, please? Just give me a solid block of rest so my body can refresh a little. I would be so grateful. Thank you, Lord. Amen."

My head sunk into the pillow and minutes later, sweet sleep enveloped me. The whimpering of a hungry baby pulled me out of dreamland and into real life.

That would be my wake up call, I silently mused. The clock displayed 4 a.m. At least she managed without me for over five hours, I couldn't really complain. It was what I asked for and I whispered my thanks to the Lord.

I got up, nursed Erin and crawled back into bed just before 5 a.m. It seemed like only five minutes went by when my alarm clock went off again. This time there was no sneaking back to bed. I had to get Nathan up, dressed, fed and off to school. I was truly grateful for the extra sleep, but still groaned, longing for the day I would be more rested. Mentally, I knew what my role of wife and mom required, but physically, I was dragging my body through each day, putting one foot in front of the other.

"Good morning, sweetie. Time for school." I gently shook Nathan awake. Krista woke up, by herself. One at a time, I sent them to the bathroom and laid out their clothes, just like I'd done so many times before. I packed lunch for Nathan, set a bowl of cereal in front of him, and supervised the loading of his backpack. I felt like the day was pulling me along. Ready or not, the morning seemed to shout in my face.

The sun was shining through the kitchen window and the sky was a vivid blue. There was moisture on the ground outside the patio door.

Did it rain? I wondered. Feeling a little worried, I asked Ruth. "Can rain affect flying conditions?"

Her answer was calm and simple. "A little rain isn't significant."

Satisfied, I shrugged it off and continued getting Nathan off to school. Once he was on his way, I nudged Krista along, changed Erin out of pajamas and into play clothes, then stopped to consider my own appearance.

Remembering that I had adult company prompted me to put on a little makeup and do something with my hair. I changed out of my sweats and into a pair of jeans and a knit top. The final outcome was more attractive and certainly more appropriate to take on the day.

The idea of fresh coffee enticed me to the kitchen. I made a pot and sipped on a cup of fresh brew as I cooked breakfast. It was a welcomed change from the previous days of childcare service, and I was enjoying the morning visiting with Ruth. The girls ate quickly and went to play.

So far, my morning was going perfectly. I offered a prayer out loud.

"Thank you God for this beautiful day and this special time to enjoy this scrumptious meal with my friend. Amen."

Ruth and I returned smiles as we enjoyed the orange juice, coffee, scrambled cheese eggs, fried potatoes, and muffins. It was worth the effort.

"Ok, *now* you can finish the famous Petersen love story!" Ruth teased.

Chapter Three:
Song in the Night

Then sings my soul, my Savior God to Thee
How great Thou art,
How great Thou art
- "How Great Thou Art" by Stuart K. Kline

We were sipping our second cup of coffee when the phone rang. It was Debbie, Dwight's secretary at the District Office. On the other end of the phone Debbie was asking me if we had heard from Rick or Dwight. The question caught me off guard.

"No," I slowly answered as my mind was beginning to sort it out. I caught myself before I went any farther. *Don't panic. Rick would say you jump to conclusions too quickly.*

Debbie immediately responded, "Well don't worry about it. But, if you hear anything, please call me."

Then I remembered Rick talked about a motel. "What about checking the motel?"

Her answer was hesitant and too quiet. "We did. They never checked in last night. They aren't at the breakfast, and the pastor scheduled to meet them at the airport waited and they never showed up."

Instantly a burst of fear flooded through my body, my voice trembled, "Well... what does that mean?"

She answered more sweetly and softer than before, "We're not sure yet, but we'll call you as soon as we know anything."

Something told me that she had already said more than she should have. I managed to thank her before I hung up the receiver. Stunned, I turned to Ruth and replayed the conversation. This was to be the first of many phone calls over a seven-hour period. Seven terribly long hours filled with questions, presumptions, guessing, fearful imaginations, and more waiting.

Ruth and I tried to keep our minds and emotions under some sense of control, but I couldn't turn off the pictures of horror as they played over and over in my mind, as if on repeat mode. The tears kept on coming with every thought and every bit of information. The most grueling thought of all was that they were out there somewhere, dead. No one knows where. Only God knows. There was absolutely nothing that we could do, but wait.

I desperately wanted to reach out to my family for some strength, comfort, and encouragement. But, since we didn't want to miss a phone call that could provide us with more information on Rick's whereabouts, we made no calls out. I could feel my body weakening and sensed I was dangerously close to the slippery slope of despair.

By this time, I was especially thankful that Ruth and I were together. At least we had each other to cling to. Instinctively we prayed. We were talking to

God from the very moment of concern, half praying, half crying out for strength. At one point, we grabbed a Bible, nervously held hands, and prayed together.

Ruth read out loud, *"The Lord is my Shepherd, I shall not be in want. He makes me lie down in green pastures, he leads me beside quiet waters, he restores my soul."*

"Oh, Ruth, read it again." I begged.

God alone had the power to hold us secure through the nightmare we were in, we instinctively knew that. Each song, each scripture we read, seemed to push the mounting fear away. It was as if a black billowing storm cloud was hovering directly over our heads, building up fury, waiting to devour us with its fatal downpour. Every time we started speculating on the possible outcome of our situation, we sang a familiar song, or read a familiar verse. We were desperately reaching for peace and comfort, literally holding on to each other for dear life.

There was a principle of faith that rang true in my heart that day in my living room. God's encouraging word directs us to worship him. All throughout Scripture we read phrases such as these: "Bow down before the Lord," "Shout to the Lord," "Sing to the Lord," "Rejoice in the Lord, always," and "Exalt the Lord with Psalms, hymns and spiritual songs."

It's not a matter of God needing recognition or praise because he's egotistical, but rather because we *need* to praise him. When God becomes the focus of our attention, the troubles and cares of this world no longer have the power to drag us down and destroy us. The Lord knows that we are prone to dwell on our problems, twisting ourselves into a pretzel of discouragement, trying to make sense of it all. He also knows that when we turn our attention away from our problem and fix our eyes on the source of our hope instead, we find rest, peace, and a reason to continue our journey.

That day, I knew I needed to refocus my attention as often as every ten minutes.

The waiting seemed to go on forever, while doubts would continue to creep into my mind. They were either dead or lost. I tried to convince myself that they were lost. *Maybe I'm over reacting because I'm already so tired and stressed out,* I told myself. *You don't know enough of the facts to make a definite conclusion. Be patient. Keep your head on.*

Ruth and I decided it would be best to keep busy with household tasks, instead of sitting around worrying. We went upstairs and methodically went from room to room fixing beds, and picking up clothes.

Suddenly, my eye caught the baby crib as I passed by the open door of Erin's bedroom. *There's a priceless picture,* I thought. Our precious baby girl, sleeping peacefully tucked in a pink blanket. I leaned my body against the door jam and drank in the "baby smell" as my mind traveled back to her birth.

I continued to be on medication the last eight weeks of my pregnancy. Sleep was hard to come by. I was restless and uncomfortable most of the time. Much of my waking hours were spent in the family room recliner, although no position was relaxing.

Finally, two weeks before my due date the doctor took me off of the medication. Immediately, I was thrown into labor and for a week I experienced around the clock contractions. We tried to end the painful ordeal by walking around. But that only made the painful contractions more frequent and longer lasting, without any progress. Exhausted, I would fall into bed, frustrated and worn ragged. After two false alarm trips to the Labor and Delivery ward of the Hospital, we were told to stay.

We were obviously anxious, yet we had all the necessary help in place. Our friend Carol would join us in labor so she could take pictures and Rick would be free to coach me. Her husband Harold would keep Krista with him and pick up Nathan from school, before bringing them to the hospital.

The labor went just like the textbooks describe. Carol made her photo shots at every stage, going through numerous rolls of film. Nothing was spared, if you know what I mean. Every vivid detail of this delivery is on film, in living color.

Rick had scratch marks on his arms where I clawed him during the final stage of labor. My transition and delivery came hard and fast, but I was able to stay on top with my breathing techniques thanks to Rick. He positioned my face looking directly into his sparkling brown eyes and his deep, calm, steady voice spoke to me. "Look at me. Look in my eyes. Our new little one is coming. You're almost there. You can do this. I'm right here. Squeeze my arm. It's OK. Look, Look. I'll breathe with you."

He began with a cleansing breath, and continued the breathing along with me until the contraction was over. The monitor clued him when the next contraction was beginning. This went on for about an hour until it was time to push. Within two hours from start to finish I gave birth to our sweet little Erin Joy.

To ensure that I had time to rest, Rick arranged for no visitors during the two days we were in the hospital. Boy, was that a blessing! I knew that once we arrived home, we had to tape up the boxes, zip up the suitcases and load the moving truck. Erin and I had plenty of bonding time and I was able to sleep a few hours in between feedings, while someone brought my meals on a tray.

The sound of a car pulling in the driveway summoned me back to the terror and anxiety awaiting me. Rushing to the upstairs bedroom window, I spotted an unfamiliar dark blue car. Ruth and I nearly collided in the hallway as we headed towards the stairs. Seeing the unexpected visitor threw us both into a panic.

Ruth screamed out, "Oh my God! It's George Wood! They sent him to tell us! I just know it!"

Her look of panic pulled me in. Hysterical, we grabbed on to each other, shouting out the ideas perking in our heads. It would make sense to send him. He was pastor to Ruth and Dwight and he knew Rick and me very well. In fact, Pastor Wood officiated our wedding.

We scrambled downstairs, still holding each other, our faces tense with fright. When we opened the door, he greeted us with his hands held up in surrender.

"I don't know any more than you do," he said. "I just wanted to come and be with you gals." Quickly, he stretched his left arm around Ruth, and right arm around me. The gripping panic dissipated as we clung to him. He didn't notice our tears staining his shirt.

George, being true to his pastor's heart, suggested that we pray. So without hesitation we joined hands making a small circle in our living room. He prayed a simple but poignant prayer as he could so aptly do, being careful to include words about God granting us strength to walk through this time of wondering and fear.

"God, be our source and comfort. Only you have the power to lift us through the storms and set our feet on solid ground. We lean on your Almighty arms. Amen."

After prayer we compared notes. There was an extensive search going on in the Tehachapi foothills area where the search and rescue team believed they would find some answers. The District Officials weren't able to give us any details until they had official word. The hope still remained that Dwight and Rick would be found, perhaps injured and unable to radio for help.

Slowly, the day moved on and pieces of the puzzle were being put together. We continued to wait. Soon the phone rang again and at Pastor George's suggestion, we let him answer it. We were so nervous and jumpy every time we heard it ring, that agreeing to George being our answering service was a relief. I can't recall which phone call it was, but I remember feeling as if someone smacked me square on the side of my head.

George's words hung in the air, "Do they have rescue helicopters at the scene? Oh I see...Just the coroner. I see." The rest of his words jumbled and a strange mental fog came over me. I heard all I needed to hear. Even after that call, officials were careful to remind us that they still did not have absolute identification of the "victims." They would only say that they found a small plane fitting the description of the one Dwight rented, and two male bodies were found inside. Repeating, "No positive identification has been made."

Just what exactly were we supposed to do with that? Of course it's them! It had to be them! That's the final piece in the puzzle. Don't they get it? Why didn't they just tell us flat out? What are they waiting for? I wanted to scream. My chest felt heavy, like the life was being sucked out of me. It hurt to breathe, and my head was pounding. *Maybe I should get in the car and drive up there?* That seemed totally irrational and crazy. *Yes, crazy. That's exactly how I feel. Like my head is not connected to my body. Maybe I've snapped. I don't know what's happening!*

Dear God please, you have to help me. I feel like I'm going to explode! Oh God. I need you! I can't do this... I can't walk through this nightmare alone.

At 4:00 p.m. they officially confirmed the names of the crash victims according to the ID found at the site. The cruel truth finally revealed that Dwight and Rick's one hour flight ended after about 25 minutes when they encountered light rain and clouds along with a high wind current which caused the plane to loose control. It apparently hit the Tehachapi foothills going full throttle. The engine was still running when the news reporters got to the scene to gather information long before we were given the final details.

One of my cousins called my mother when he heard the evening news reporting the crash of a small plane. He couldn't believe his ears when "victim, Rick Petersen" was announced on the television airwaves. My mother, in shock, called me immediately. The conversation was brief. I told her the brutal details through the sobs as she assured me that she and Dad were packing and on their way.

More phone calls poured in. "I can't believe what I heard." "Tell me it isn't true." Then I realized that we had to contact Rick's parents who were Missionaries in Africa, and his sisters, in Minnesota. It was looming in my mind to call or telegram his parents and tell them.

Rick's Uncle Dick and Aunt Ellen pastored a church nearby and came to my rescue with in a few hours. Not only were they there for moral support but they also helped me with the difficult task of contacting family and friends. I couldn't be tied to the phone; I had to take care of my children. Once they made the initial key calls, word of the tragedy spread like a wild fire. It didn't take long.

Things and faces seemed to blur around me, yet I kept moving. The pain began as a kind of stabbing, gut-wrenching blow. When it struck, it immediately took my breath away and sent a cold sweat all over my body, flowing out of my eyes in a stream of tears. My mind tried desperately to cling to some kind of reasoning, but the cold, hard truth overpowered everything else.

You know that sinking sensation you feel during a roll-a-coaster ride? Take that and add the symptoms resembling the flu. Weak, sick to your stomach, light-headed, flashes of hot then cold. There is no way to know when it's coming. There's no way to stop it or

prepare for it. It just comes without warning and
you weep, weakening with every wave of grief. The
moment you feel like you're under control, someone
asks, "Have you heard from Rick's parents yet?" Or
the phone rings, and there it goes again.

It was torture! Everything in me wanted to reject
it. *I hate this. I hate how I feel.* I hated what was
happening. It didn't matter how hard I resisted. I
was completely powerless.

Pastors, friends, and family began to drop by.
In a mind-fog I stopped what I was doing to hug
and cry with each one as they tried to comfort me,
and somehow I drew strength from them. By early
evening we realized that this had gone on for hours.

One friend stopped by and asked if we had eaten.
The only reason I felt compelled to respond to him
was because other people were around encouraging
me.

"No, we haven't eaten since breakfast, and yes,
food would be a good idea." I admit we were beginning
to feel the effects of the ordeal. It was physically and
emotionally draining.

He slipped out quietly and later returned laden
down with buckets of chicken, salads, rolls and liters
of soft drinks. The smell of fried chicken captured
my senses long enough to interest me in a few bites.
We fed the children and made a plate for ourselves.
Visiting family and friends joined us as we sat in
shock, half dazed, while the house continued to fill
with guests.

The pressure in my head was mounting. *It must
be from all the crying*, I thought. I turned to Ruth, "I
need an aspirin. How about you?"

"Oh yes, that sounds great," she said, quietly. "My head is pounding.

"I'll be right back," I whispered and then headed for the medicine cabinet.

For the first time in several hours, I made my way out of the living room, through the crowd and up the stairs to our bedroom. I felt strangely light-headed, as if I was watching myself from somewhere outside of my body.

Immediately upon entering our room I sensed a curious presence that intensified as I walked by Rick's open closet. *There, there it is.... That heart-sinking feeling again!* Enveloped in a cold sweat, I could feel the growing lump in my throat slowly choking me. I broke down into tears. By the time I reached the vanity in the bathroom my hands landed with a slap on the counter as my body trembled and knees buckled under me. It was as if I was being wrenched by some unknown power. I couldn't see or hear it, but I sure felt it! What was worse, I had no control over my emotions.

By now I was shaking uncontrollably and barely able to stand. Paralyzed by grief, I forgot why I was standing there. The pain in my head intensified as I cried. My exploding headache brought me back to the reason I was there and I remembered the aspirin. Looking up, I saw a reflection in the mirror.

"Dear God... help me," I whispered.

There, standing hunched over was a pathetic young woman staring back at me. "Look at you," I sputtered. "Your eyes are all red and puffy, and your face all blotchy. What a sad mess you are! What's happening to you? Someone please help her! Will someone please rescue this poor, poor woman?"

I collapsed to my knees and cried out in gut-wrenching pain, "I want my husband. Bring him to me!"

Sobbing, with my head in my hands I cried out again in anguish, "I want my Rick! Please come home Rick. This has got to be a mistake. Someone please tell me it's not true. Please, please... it's not TRUE! It can't be! Oh God, Oh God, please help me!"

Chapter Four:
Standing on Faith

"On Christ the solid rock I stand
All other ground is sinking sand"
- The Solid Rock by Edward Mote and
William B. Bradbury

Beyond tired, my body was drained from sobbing and wrenched from the emotional strain. Still, my mind would not shut down and I had no desire to go back to bed. Every time I went to sleep, I ended up dreaming of a smoky twin-engine plane, its crumpled hull damaged beyond recognition. Always, I'd awake, yearning for his touch. Rolling over in bed with eyes still closed, I'd begin the motions of familiar cuddling with my husband, only to be startled by a cold empty sheet.

For the longest time after Rick's death, one of the hardest times to endure was the nighttime. After the lights went out and I surrendered to sleep, fear crept into my room. Replays of foggy scenes over and over in my sub-conscience left me feeling ripped off.

In one such dream, I was in the kitchen cooking dinner and the house was dark and dreary, and packed with family and friends deep in conversation. Suddenly, there was a commotion at the front door, and the crowd moved in to see what all the noise was about. I was in the back of the room, straining to see what was going on. There, in the sunlight of the open door, stood Rick, smiling and greeting those around him.

Someone asked, "Where have you been all this time? Why didn't you call or write?" Others cried and reached for hugs.

Shocked and exuberant, I pushed my way through the crowd toward my dear sweet husband, the love of my life, whom I missed desperately. But there were too many people blocking my path. There was no way to reach him. Waving my arms frantically, I cried out, "Rick! Rick.... Hon...it's me! I'm here! Look back here!"

He never saw me and never made eye contact.

Sometimes, in the dream he would look right at me, smile, and then turn around back into the sunlight, slipping away from sight. Other times, I would somehow reach him, though there was always an exhausting struggle that left me weak and frustrated. He would extend his arms to me, giving me a hug and perhaps a quick kiss, all the while maintaining that familiar smile. But it was never anything more than that. And then, as quickly as he came into my dream, he left.

As the years progressed, I asked him why he was gone for so long and where he had been. My voice became surprisingly gutsy as I reprimanded him for not calling me or helping with the kids.

I pushed him away, yelling, "It's too late now! I needed you when the kids were little. It's too late now. I'm married to someone else. You can't just waltz back into my life like nothing happened, you know!"

Each time I would wake up disturbed by the cruel reality. The gut-wrenching grief of earlier days sucked me in and tears drenched my pillow. My life was forever changed. I couldn't hold onto him, the life that we shared, our marriage, any of it.

My dreams shook me to the core, clearly telling me that somewhere deep inside I was still wishing and hoping for what used to be. Day in and day out, I forced myself to push aside the memory of Rick so that I could live in the present with a sense of joy and peace. I knew that my children needed Mom fully alive and functioning in the present, not the past. But, at night when the lights went out, my imprisoned hopes would emerge.

I don't dare call them dreams, because *dream* is too nice of a word. They were nightmares! Rick's sweet caress or gentle touch that I so desperately longed for didn't satisfy me one bit. And the harsh cruel reality was that even though I wished and hoped all night long, the morning sun would surely rise and expose the raw truth. *"I was alone and my Rick was gone."*

One night, after I awoke from one of those haunting dreams, I decided to stay awake. I knew my mind would inevitably try to sift through the turmoil that was whirling around in my mind if I went to sleep.

So after nursing Erin and putting her back in her crib, I stepped into my slippers, threw a sweatshirt around my shoulders, grabbed my journal and pen, and pulled my Bible onto my lap.

"Lord, speak to me." I prayed. "I feel myself sinking...as if I'm a little row boat out on the vast ocean and a storm is whipping all around me. I'm completely defenseless. I'm afraid to take one step, even one tiny tiptoe step without you, Father. You are my anchor, my only hope."

I could feel a battle raging inside me. My soul and my spirit were playing tug-of-war for my attention. My soul wanted to give up more than anything to escape the pain, fear and despair. But my spirit held me steady. It accepted the challenge of the battle, taking a stance against the crushing weight of the loss.

Out of my spirit, I began to sing hymns of glorious praise to God. It was amazing to me that during some of my darkest hours of mental anguish and physical draining, my voice was exalting God. It seemed a little strange. After all, how could I be giving God praise when my husband was just killed?

The words that came to my mind arising from my spirit were strengthening. I would sing songs like this one.

> *His oath, his covenant, his blood*
> *Support me in the whelming flood*
> *When all around my soul gives way,*
> *He then is all my hope and stay* [1]

That's exactly how I felt, like my soul was "giving way," sinking into a mysterious hole of despair. In my mind, I could see myself desperately rowing a boat, frantically beating the waves with my pitiful oars in a vain attempt to fight against the powerful winds and driving rain. Then, as I slowly began to utter the words of the hymn, unexplainable warmth poured over me. Singing it over and over, I was lost in an oasis of comfort.

On Christ the solid rock I stand
All other ground is sinking sand [1]

I would run there for strength—every hour on the hour if need be, until the fire of panic and fear was quenched. My spirit drove me forward to embrace the words of Scripture, set to musical praise in songs and hymns. In the midst of my pain and suffering, I found I needed the comfort of my Lord the most.

One of my favorite authors, Chuck Swindoll, explains suffering so well in his book, *For Those Who Hurt.*

> Suffering reveals our creature status. We are not all wise or infinite in strength. But God is. And we need Him – we were created to need Him. Desperately. Sometimes it takes coming to the end of one's self to see that. God knows. We need to take everything we were, everything we are and everything we've ever hoped to be and simply place it all in the nail-scarred hands of our loving Lord. And lean hard on His Word. [2]

And that's exactly what I did. One of the first passages in the Bible that I "leaned hard" on was Romans 8:26:

> *Likewise the Spirit also helps in our* **weaknesses***. For we do not know what we should pray for as we ought, but the Spirit Himself makes intercession for us with groanings which cannot be uttered.*

When I read these words, I couldn't help but see that there is help for the weak. I was definitely in a place of weakness and in my brokenness I had no idea how to pray. I struggled to put words together that made any sense at all. Most of the time, I would give up trying. I'd just sit and cry my eyes out, sobbing before the Lord, helpless and sad. These words, and many others in Scripture, gave me permission to cry, sob, and even despair because the Spirit Himself *makes intercession* for *me.*

Romans 8, goes on to say in verse 27: "*Now He who searches the hearts knows what the mind of the Spirit is, because He makes* **intercession** *for the saints according to the will of God.*"

The Spirit of God intercedes for me—one of the "saints," according to the definition in this Scripture—by directing my prayers. The Lord was the anchor that held me steady in my storm. Even if I feel weak and helpless, God is NOT weak or helpless, ever. My assurance comes from knowing that the Spirit of God helps the weak by interceding according to the Father's will.

The next verse I was about to read was hard to swallow at first. Truthfully, I rejected it right off the bat. I wanted to end the passage with verse 27, but I knew better. As a student of God's Word, I knew I needed to read the entire passage and then interpret the message as a whole in context. Romans 8:28, says, *"And we know that all things work together for good to those who love God, to those who are the called according to His purpose."* NKJV

At first, I argued against in disbelief. *For Good? Who are we kidding? What good could possibly come out of my husband dying? He was father to three young children. Can you tell me what's good about children growing up without their daddy? Don't talk to me about good!*

This is where my faith displayed its true colors. There was absolutely NO way this side of Heaven that I could conjure up a palatable explanation of good for my situation. There was none. But, that's the key here. I had no way of seeing past my crushing pain. If God had shown me His complete plan for my life right then, I wouldn't have bought it. I would probably have insisted that I was loosing my mind and checked myself into a funny farm.

Faith makes no demands to *know* or even understand. Faith, by its very nature, *trusts* without understanding. You may be thinking that it's too hard to trust when you're desperate to make sense of chaos. And you're right. It is hard and probably impossible—unless your faith and hope is in someone greater than yourself.

My faith didn't just show up one day and introduce itself perfectly developed and rock solid. Faith is a journey. Here's another quote from Chuck Swindoll's book that speaks to this point:

We cannot prepare for a crisis after the crisis occurs. Preparation must take place before we are nose to nose with the issue. Sometimes we are barely keeping balance on the spiritual tightrope as we are... then something shakes the rope! Disaster blows in the door. [2]

We make an initial decision to begin our journey of faith when we accept Christ as our Lord and Savior. And that's just the beginning. At the moment of salvation, our faith is like a seed. It must grow and become strong and vibrant, because if it doesn't, it will never hold through life's storms.

Chuck goes on to say: "In other words, the real *test* of your spiritual stability does not come while your little pond is free from ripples. It comes when the waves of suffering roll in."[3]

Before Rick died, my little pond was free from ripples, and my preparation for that crisis occurred years before. My response to his death became the testing ground that "proved" my faith. In a nutshell, all of my experiences growing up—the aches and pains, the struggle of discovering myself, developing a spiritual backbone, and putting muscle to my faith— shaped me into a woman whose spirit remained steady while I was suffering great loss.

How did I stand? I was able to endure the stormy blast of grief because I was *built* to hold to my faith. It's not that I was such a strong person, Lord knows, I wasn't. Even today, I still don't consider myself strong by any measure. Therein, rests the beauty of this truth. It's not the measure of our strength that's important, but our reliance on God's strength.

When the principles of God's Word are instilled into you at an early age, you are trained to walk by *faith*. The Word teaches that it is by his Spirit that we are strengthened and empowered to keep going.

I'm not saying that I didn't grapple with the "why?" question. Everyone does and I was no exception. But, I didn't pitch a tent in the land of the unknown, like so many do. I had been a Christian for a long time and understood all too well that even if I could get the answer to that question, it wouldn't diminish my pain. My husband would still be in Heaven and my children and I would still be here on Earth without their daddy.

I knew instinctively when this disaster hit that it was a testing of my faith. There was no discussion or arguing, no choosing on my part. I was being placed in the fire of suffering, like gold being purified by flames. There was no question in my mind that I had to clench tenaciously to the teachings of God's word in order to survive the heat and to get through such a time of great testing. In order to have full recovery from my wounds, it would require me to be solely dependent on God.

A friend of ours, Doug Dennee, recently underwent hip replacement surgery. He described his recovery process to me.

"Well, I'm not taking as much pain medication as I did immediately following surgery, which is evidence of progress," he said, "and, I'm going in for physical therapy three times a week, which will taper off to once a week. I am even making headway on my daily exercises; but I have some good days, and some I want to just stay in bed. But, overall, I'm seeing improvement so I'm feeling optimistic!"

I've never had major surgery like that, but I understand what the recovery process entails. In the same way a physical wound needs care and recovery, the damage caused by emotional pain also needs this process of rehabilitation. My heart had been torn apart and badly needed mending, which is why I spent so much time alone with God. I reminded myself, *he is the Great Physician, and the only source of hope and healing for my life.* That much I knew for sure.

Below is a passage that helped me during my process of recovery. I've highlighted the words that gave me strength.

> *For God, who said, "Let light shine out of darkness," made his light shine in our hearts to give us the light of the knowledge of the glory of God in the face of Christ. But we have this treasure in jars of clay to show that this all-surpassing power is from God and not from us. We are hard pressed on every side, but not crushed; perplexed, but not in despair; persecuted, but not abandoned, struck down, but not destroyed. Therefore,* **we do not lose heart***. Though outwardly we are wasting away, yet inwardly we are being renewed day by day. For our light and momentary troubles are achieving for us an eternal glory that far outweighs them all.* **So we fix our eyes not on what is seen.** *For what is seen is temporary, but what is unseen is eternal.* (2 Corinthians 4:6-9, 16-18)

Standing my Ground

Do you ever wonder why the Bible is called the "Sword of the Spirit?" Ephesians 6:17, says: *"Take the helmet of salvation and the sword of the Spirit, which is the word of God."*

God's Word is called a sword because the Bible is a spiritual weapon. In Hebrews 4:12, it says:

> *For the word of God is living and active and sharper than any two-edged sword, and piercing as far as the division of soul and spirit, of both joints and marrow, and able to judge the thoughts and intentions of the heart.*

You might ask why we need a spiritual weapon. Physical battles are fought with physical weapons, but spiritual battles are fought with spiritual weapons. Makes sense, doesn't it?

"For though we live in the world, we do not wage war as the world does. The weapons we fight with are not the weapons of the world. On the contrary, they have divine power to demolish strongholds." (2 Corinthians 10:3-4)

Think about it. Spiritual battles occur when we are completely spent and feeling exhausted, when the enemy can attack and probably do serious damage. Why? It's because our physical bodies are weak, and therefore vulnerable.

Whenever I read these verses in 2 Corinthians, it strikes me as profound that there is a real enemy out there whose sole objective is to kill—and his sights are fixed on me. We are engaged in a spiritual battle that is waged on everyone that follows after Jesus and calls himself or herself a "Christian." I know this to be true because the Bible speaks a lot about the war between the devil and God. It's all throughout Scripture, from Genesis to Revelation. But besides this, I understand it to be true in my own life.

Jesus says, *"The thief comes only to steal, kill and destroy; I have come that they may have life, and have it to the full."* (John 10:10) In this passage, Jesus is saying that Satan, the archenemy of God will stop at nothing to steal from me, a child of God. He will attempt to threaten, frighten, rip me apart piece by piece, and ultimately destroy me.

What I stood on during those times of attack was my faith. I actively believed that my hope and future rested in God's hands, not Satan's. The longer I looked at my situation in the way God's Word viewed it, the more hope and strength I found, because God's Word is life-giving. I am still reminded of this truth every day.

The battle raging inside me was spiritual and it affected every part of me: my body, my soul (comprised of the mind, will, intellect and emotions), and my spirit. At first, when I was in a state of shock, I was too confused and wounded to analyze what was happening. Then, the more I studied the Bible, the more I realized that all through his Word, God was teaching me all about my true identity in Christ.

As Christians, we are "Soldiers of God," and as such we should expect trouble and attacks in this life. What soldier would dress for battle, get equipped with a weapon and full gear, and then act surprised and confused when fired upon? Doesn't that sound ridiculous? That's the picture that came to my mind as I read the verses in the Bible about spiritual warfare.

I probably read them many times before, but never did they make such an impact on me until Rick was killed. Everything about it felt like a ruthless enemy attack. A deadly scud missile exploded into my life and devastated me completely. My life as I knew it was over and I was left to oversee the recovery, cleanup and rebuilding process. Nothing about it was simple or "fair" and everyday presented a monumental task of placing one foot in front of the other. Sometimes stumbling, I dragged myself forward inch by inch.

I would definitely have to agree with Pastor Chuck Swindoll. I had to lean hard on the word of God for help through the "attack-recovery." As I began to adopt a more militant mindset I also began taking on my life much like a soldier approaches war. Although I had no military knowledge per se, I imagined the necessary requirements and disciplines a soldier's daily routine involved, and made some changes in my everyday life. For instance, soldiers never whine and fuss about how hard it is, right? I changed my thinking from believing I was a "victim" to behaving like a "soldier." Big difference.

Faith That's Tested... Grows

If there's one thing that a true soldier knows, it's that just because something is "hard" or difficult, doesn't mean it's "bad." As a child, I understood "hard." At school I was teased for being shorter than everyone else and wearing out-dated, hand-me-down clothes. I fought for the B's and C's I received and no matter how hard I tried, I strained to keep up with the rest of the class.

Riding along with the "hard," or difficult, was the "good." The good was the value system that I was raised with. The first thing I learned was that Jesus loved me. The second thing was that I was never going to be perfect enough to make it to Heaven on my own. The best news of all was that Jesus died in my place so that I could have a relationship with my Father God and live forever with him. When I accepted Christ as my Personal Savior, I became a member in a much larger family—the Family of God.

I grew up in a home of simple means, but we were rich by God's standards. Our home was filled with evidence of Christian influence, with Christian Bible teachers over the radio, Christian music both live and recorded, and regular on-your-knees prayer meetings. Any time the church doors were open, our family was there! My parents served in the church faithfully and as soon as we were old enough, my siblings and I did too.

In Sunday school, I learned songs that were played over and over. This music was key to infusing courage and truth into my young spirit by strengthening me and causing me to mature spiritually. We also studied and memorized Bible passages relentlessly in order to win game prizes. I can't even count the number of verses that we committed to memory. We sang simple songs with huge promises like:

Jesus loves me, this I know
For the Bible tells me so
Little ones to Him belong
They are weak but He is strong
- Anna B. Warner, William B. Bradbury

During my battles with grief, the Bible verses that were planted so many years ago welled up from inside me and filled my soul with strength and peace. I knew in my heart that God was worth trusting regardless of how I felt or how difficult my crisis. The strength that I exhibited wasn't my own, but it was a direct result of my confidence in God. Romans 10:17 says, *"...faith comes from hearing the message, and the message is heard through the word of Christ."*

My God has never failed yet, because he is true to his word and he cannot fail. Some other Scripture that attests to this:

"Trust in the Lord with all your heart and lean not on your own understanding, in all your ways acknowledge him – and he will direct your paths." (Proverbs 3:5,6 NKJV)

"And my God will meet all your needs, according to his glorious riches in Christ Jesus." (Philippians 4:19)

"I can do all things through Christ who strengthens me. (Philippians 4:13 NKJV)

These and other verses took root in my spirit. I didn't fully understand all that each one meant,

but the more I studied, the hungrier I became to
know God in a deeper way. Can you see how God,
the Master Designer, took the pieces of my life and
shaped and molded me into something that he could
use?

Looking back, I can see how piece by piece, bit
by bit, God was building my spirit, or my *faith* to
be strong and healthy. The years spent training in
"faith walking" as a child and young teen were what
saved me from drowning in my darkest hour.

A defining moment for me in those tender years
of learning how to walk by faith came one evening
when God pointed his finger at me while attending
a special church service. As a young teenage girl I
felt as if he had branded his love for people onto my
heart. During the message, a missionary speaker
asked, "If you feel that God is calling you to be a
missionary, step out from your seat and walk to the
front of the sanctuary."

People from all directions were making their way
to the front. My heart was moved. *He's talking to
me!* I felt a burning deep within my soul and an
indescribable force drawing me forward, bringing me
before the platform with wide-eyed anticipation. I
sensed that it was to be one of those pivotal moments
in my life. As hands of elders and church leaders
were placed on each one of us in the circle, deliberate,
earnest prayers were raised to the heavens on our
behalf. Prayers carrying prophetic implications were
released that day.

One of the missionaries slowly turned to me
after the prayer, and looked carefully into my eyes.
Smiling, he whispered. "You have a very special call

for service on your life, young lady. Are you willing to go wherever God sends you?"

He seemed concerned that I fully understood the implications of his question.

There was no doubt in my mind that God was speaking to me, but I did have doubts about myself. *Could I possibly be good enough for God to use? Do I have what it takes to serve in ministry selflessly without complaint or question?*

Suddenly a sinking feeling struck me and I resisted. *Just look at me! I'm nobody special. I have no flashy talent, no impressive gifts to offer. Even God would have his work cut out if he wanted to use me?*

Then my thoughts turned a corner. *But, if God sees me just as I am and still chooses me for his service...if this is his design for me, then how can I say no?*

With a renewed strength, I blurted out, "Yes, oh yes, I'm willing. I want to go wherever he needs me."

That night, my faith soared to a new height and my commitment to serve God was stronger than ever.

That event was a turning point for me. Inwardly, my spiritual life began to flourish as I attempted to follow the plan God had in mind for me. Outwardly, I was becoming more confident. The awkward shy little girl was becoming an independent young lady. The biggest challenge left for me to tackle was to finish growing up.

Endless Daily Battles

In the days after Rick's death, the constant battle between my soul and my spirit continued. In the beginning, when the grief was fresh and my emotions were still raw, it was an hourly fight. But as time went on, the battles became less frequent and less intense.

Just like after a major surgery, my recovery was very shaky at first. But obediently I put to practice what I *knew* to be true and rejected thoughts of fear and despair.

I remember one warm August evening when I was sitting at my dining room table, staring at my checkbook balance. Knowing full well that there wasn't enough to get us through the month, I quoted out loud, making it personal: *"And my God will meet all **my** needs according to his glorious riches in Christ Jesus."*

I was exercising my faith and praying back to God what his Word promised me. The next Sunday, my pastor slipped a check into my hand, given anonymously by someone in the congregation. That month and every month, our bills were paid, our needs were met, and there was always plenty of food on the table.

Another time my faith was tested was when our youngest, Erin Joy, at the age of 15 months underwent surgery. Her tiny body was plagued with chronic ear infections for months and after trying one medication after another, the doctor offered to place a set of tubes in her ears. I don't know if you can imagine what it's like to sit in the recovery room while your baby is in surgery, but let me tell you, it's not fun. I cried and prayed the whole time, wishing her daddy was there with me. For hours after surgery, I cried and prayed, rocking Erin in my arms. I knew God was there and his "voice" comforted me through that time of helplessness.

For years, Erin underwent several more surgeries, multiple procedures and doctor's visits, as we sought healing for her little body. It was grueling and challenging to say the least, but we made it through by God's power and help.

Besides the battles with finances and Erin's health, we had legal issues to face due to the nature of the plane crash. Not to mention, our children also struggled with issues relating to the loss of a father, and were challenged with other issues typical to teenagers growing up.

I know that God hears and answers prayers because he sent me tangible real life assistance during that first year, especially during that rocky life-threatening part. God heard my cries for help and sent my older sister, Joy, to move in with me. After Rick's death, she quit her job, packed up her belongings and became my roommate. Her experience as a pediatric nurse and her keen attention to detail saved me on many occasions. I also had a dear family friend who came over about once a week and played with the kids while I read a book or went out to dinner with a friend.

After that first year, I was on my own more or less, and it was even more difficult. But, just when I would get discouraged, something happened that would lift me up.

For example, one summer afternoon several weeks after the kids and I moved back to San Diego into a small three-bedroom house, I was outside trying my best to mow the front lawn. Notice I said *trying*, because as you can probably guess, I never had to mow our lawn before Rick died. He always took care of the yard work. Knowing that I couldn't afford to pay someone to do it and my oldest child was only eight years old, I was determined to manicure the yard myself. After repeated sputtering the mower finally started, but when I stopped to empty the bag, the motor died. Over and over I pulled the cord, exhausting my strength and patience. I wanted to kick the thing, but instead burst into tears.

"Great! I sobbed. "This is just great! My lawn has a Mohawk, and I can't get this stupid piece of tin to start up again. Where's my husband? He could get it going."

My cousin, Debbie, happened to be driving by at the same time and immediately identified my dilemma. Secretly, she arranged for a gardener to come regularly and tend to our lawn. She didn't ask me, she just knew that I needed a gift of compassion right about then and mercifully relieved me of that frustrating chore. I was elated, to say the least.

These are a few examples of how God heard my cries. He didn't take me out of the trouble, but using tenderhearted friends and loved ones, he led me through it. I'm sharing these examples to show you that I continued to live in the real world. Whether I felt equipped or not, life danced on and I had to pick myself up each time I felt like quitting and get a grip. Thankfully, others around me were willing and able to step forward, making my job somewhat manageable.

Today, as I write these words, I'm happily married to a wonderful Christian man who supports me in every way. Once again, my life is filled with romance and intimacy, like I never thought possible. It's just like God to take our broken pieces and make something beautiful out of them. He has worked out his plan in my life, even through times where I've made mistakes or followed my own desires. Through it all, he's remained faithful. He doesn't require perfection from his children, just obedience.

I'm not sure where I would be or what subsequent disasters my life would have produced had I not possessed a genuine faith in God. I've walked through the valley during Rick's death and still continue my journey of Faith, by the life-empowering and soul-sustaining weapon of truth, God's word to us, the Bible.

God keeps his word. He is more than able to take care of every one of his children. My faith in God that was established many years before was tested in a crucible of heart-wrenching agony. Everyday I made a choice to fix my eyes on the truth of God's word, and not on the things around me that were not eternal.

Struggles, crises and challenges have continued to be obstacles in my life, but God has led me through each one. I have been attacked, threatened, and crushed, but NOT destroyed because my God is greater than any other power or force, and my faith and hope was anchored in HIM. I continue to place my trust and confidence in Him, regardless of how difficult the road.

Chapter Five:
God's Invitation

"The sun has not ceased shining because the traveler through the tunnel has ceased to see it."
- *The Christian's Secret of a Happy Life*, by Hannah Whitall Smith.

As you read my story, you may have been saying, "this sounds unreal. How does someone go through this caliber of suffering and not shake her fist at God? That's just not normal."

Rick held the theology credentials, not me, but I can share some biblically based reasoning that helped me through my time of intense testing. Early on in my journey of faith, I realized that God's word was much too big for me to fully comprehend. There have been many times that I've asked God challenging questions, and though I may have been kicking and screaming during these seasons of pain and confusion, I didn't "blame" God.

The way I see it, we live in this fallen world with its sin and destruction ravaging souls everywhere. The mere fact that I live in this troubled place, subjects me to trouble. Knowing that God is bigger than my circumstances gives me hope much like a life preserver holds a swimmer's head above water. In the same way, although my faith kept me from drowning, it didn't take me out of the water.

I admit there were numerous times when I felt like throwing in the towel. Many times I wanted to take a long vacation all by myself and let someone else take care of things at home. But, each time I felt that way, I snuggled up in my Father God's lap and asked for help. He would hold me close, whisper assurances into my ear, and give me the strength to make it through another day or two, or three.

No, I wasn't physically in his lap, of course. It was during those times I would receive a poem or verse that would lift me up. Or, I would receive an unexpected visit from a Christian friend and we would spend several invaluable hours in fellowship together. This boosted me for weeks. Another time, I received a book with a message of hope, like I trust this one is for you.

My Anchor, My Hope

Although I wish this part of my life didn't exist, I can't remove the pain and suffering from my life any more than you can remove it from yours. We don't have the luxury of choosing to accept only the fun and enjoyable times and rejecting the painful times. We can, however choose how we walk *through* this life—with the good, the bad, and the ugly.   I chose and continue to choose to give every bit of my life to God, because he is the anchor that holds me steady.

The other part of this means, that God also has the controls of my life. He's the pilot and, at best, I'm the co-pilot. That's the most logical choice, isn't it? After all, he is the One who knows the beginning from the end. I don't. As long as I surrender to God's work and plan in my life, I'm safe and protected and enjoy all the promises in God's word. That's how I rest secure! That is the only way I can sleep—in his arms.

It doesn't matter who you are or what title you hold, you need an anchor in order to make it through this life on earth. For me, it was and is God—in His word and His character is where my hope lies. In Hannah Whitall Smith's book, *The Christian's Secret of a Happy Life*, she writes:

> Let your faith, then, throw its arms around all God has told you, and in every dark hour remember that though now for a season, if need be, you are in heaviness through manifold temptations, it is only like going through a tunnel. The sun has not ceased shining because the traveler through the tunnel has ceased to see it; and the Sun of righteousness is still shining, although you in your dark tunnel do not see Him. Be patient and trustful and wait. This time of darkness is only permitted that the trial of your faith, being much more precious than of gold that perishes though it be tried

with fire, might be found unto praise
and honor and glory at the appearing of
Jesus Christ.[3]

I love this wonderful woman of faith even though I
don't know her personally, because her writing often
ignites a spark of hope in me and points me to the
truth. Too often, I'm the traveler in the dark tunnel,
impatient and restless, wondering what happened to
the sun! So much of my time is spent entertaining
thoughts that are destructive rather than life giving.
Thoughts like, *I'm a disappointment to God,* or *my
kids are going to be ruined because of me,* or *I've
made too many mistakes, God can't use me.*

The idea of testing is to see what shines through
on the other side. What you truly believe is revealed
in times of suffering. I will choose to believe what
God says, not what I think, or what someone else
thinks. The most powerful lesson I learned during
my stormy rowboat days continues to be the greatest
lesson of all time: *"God loves me."* Though I may
have felt battered and bruised, when I surveyed the
damage and all the evidence around me proved bleak
and sorrowful, the bottom line remained solid. God
loved me and He always will.

His love was strong enough to conquer my pain,
regardless of how I *felt.* Feelings are not required
to embrace *faith.* What is more important here is
that real faith ignores emotions and cuts right to the
truth. Truth is unchanging. God's Word is truth—in
its purest form, which is why I chose and continue to
choose faith over feelings.

Here's a great passage that's packed with soul-
strengthening assurance.

> *Who shall separate us from the love*
> *of Christ? Shall trouble, or hardship or*
> *persecution, or famine or nakedness, or*
> *danger or sword? ...No, in all these things*
> *we are more than conquerors through him*
> *who loved us. For I am convinced that*
> *neither death or life, neither angels nor*
> *demons, neither the present, nor the future,*
> *neither height nor depth, nor anything else*
> *in all creation, will be able to separate us*
> *from the love of God that is in Christ Jesus*
> *our Lord.* (Romans 8:35-39)

Now I will personalize this passage so that it applies more directly to my situation. As I read these words, I pictured myself crawling up into my Daddy-God's lap where He's holding me. Look at this promise!

Who shall separate me from the love of Christ?
Shall pain, or stress, or confusion, or heart-break, or
loneliness or fatigue? No! In all these things I am more
than a conqueror through Him who loved me. Yes,
I am convinced that neither my death, Rick's death,
or my life, nor angels, nor Satan, nor powers, nor
things around me now or in the future, nor mountain
or valley, nor any other created thing, shall be able
to steal the love of God away from me. For it is given
to me through Christ Jesus my Lord, and He is my
secure anchor in the middle of the storm. Yes!

Those midnight battles that would last anywhere from thirty minutes to three hours were grueling and heart breaking of course, but the next time I was in one it wasn't as difficult to get through, because I was better prepared. Reading and believing the Scripture gave me a priceless reward of peace, covering me like a blanket. Eventually, I had no trouble falling asleep. When I closed my eyes I saw Jesus holding children in his arms, and holding young mothers in his arms. A warm assurance spread over me and I was able to rest knowing that everything was going to be OK.

It's just as true today, you know. Yes, Jesus loves me. And He loves you. You can believe it too, the Bible tells us so.

Perhaps you were not raised in a Christian home and right now you are facing a crisis that seems unbearable. It's never too late to place your life in God's hands. He is the Creator, and he can create something beautiful out of whatever brokenness, pain or mess you may find yourself in. Trust me, *I know.* You can begin your walk of faith today, and find the strength to bear what seems humanly impossible.

You can choose Jesus as your anchor of hope, or you can try to handle life's challenges on your own. That's up to you. But, my prayer is that you will see through the example of my life, just how vital a relationship with Jesus Christ is. He is the Savior that saves us from eternal death, the compassionate one who picks us up when we are knocked down, and rescues us from all the messes we get ourselves into.

Through faith in Jesus Christ and making him Lord of your life, you will have lasting hope—for every situation, crisis, tragedy or heartache. When you place your complete trust in him, you will discover that He alone is strong enough to carry you through this life with all its crazy twists and turns.

Although you may search, you will never find anything in this world as certain, as reliable, and as life changing as God's Word. His Word lovingly presents us with the gift and knowledge of his Son, Jesus Christ. Even though man has chosen sin and as a consequence is separated from God, the Lord already made amends for our mistakes in the past, present and future. Since the beginning of time at the foundations of the world, he foreknew you and had a plan for your life.

Patiently waiting for us to invite him in, God stands before the door to our hearts and knocks. Will you let him in, today? Jesus Christ is the greatest gift this world has ever known, and his hand of invitation is extended to all who will receive him. When you accept the gift of salvation that was provided by the atoning blood of Jesus Christ, you become a new person from the inside out. The Spirit of God will come and dwell in you bringing peace, love, joy, patience, hope and so much more.

I chose Jesus as the source of my hope many years ago. God rescued me as a young frightened child, instilled his Word in my heart, and carried me through the darkest hour of my life. It is only by his constant pouring of grace and love over me that I am able to write this message of hope to you—all because of who he is, and not because of who I am or anything that I have done or could do. I cannot earn the full right and privilege of being a Child of God. I am his adopted child simply because I have believed and confessed that Christ died for my sins and for the sins of the whole world so that we could have a full, unhindered relationship with the Almighty God.

This relationship is continuous and will deepen for the rest of our lives here on Earth and for all eternity.

What is Your Answer to Christ?

If you have not yet begun your journey of faith, will you take the first step today? I pray that my story illustrates the eternal value of a personal relationship with Jesus Christ, and that today you will see how God has provided a vehicle to rescue you from life's dead end road. Not only has he provided a rescue but he has also designed a way for you and me to spend eternity with him. God's promises are eternal. Isn't that amazing?

Here's what the Bible says about it. *"For God so loved the world that he gave his one and only Son, that whoever believes in him shall not perish but have eternal life."* (John 3:16) And: *"For the wages of sin is death, but the gift of God is eternal life, in Christ Jesus our Lord."* (Romans 6:23)

God demonstrated in a dramatic way how much he loves us, his prize creation, when he sent his only son to die in our place. These verses tell us that we are all sentenced to eternal death because of sin. But, our loving God established a plan that offers a "way out" for anyone who believes in Him, AND accepts his gift of salvation through his son Jesus Christ.

It is as if I was standing in a court of law, having just been sentenced to life in prison and this man, Jesus, steps up and says, "I'll pay the full penalty for this woman's crime, she is free from this judgment. Release her."

Can you imagine that? That's exactly what Jesus accomplished by dying on the cross. He paid the penalty for all of the sins of mankind.

The challenge for some is realizing that we are all sinners. Some people don't want to accept that fact but it's still true. When sin entered the world through the transgression of one man, Adam, every person on the planet inherited the consequences of their disobedience. This initial sin caused a breach in the relationship between God and mankind.

But God continued to reach out to his prize creation. Think about it. He made us in HIS image and his deep love for us found a way to rescue us from destruction. All we have to do is believe in him and accept the gift of salvation. It sounds simple doesn't it? Actually it is rather simple. But, simple doesn't mean "easy."

I won't sugar coat it—living a life of faith in God takes a great deal of commitment and perseverance. We are still human and along with that human nature is the desire to please our flesh. We struggle with temptations to be greedy, selfish and rebellious. But we must remember that with this great blessing also comes a great deal of responsibility. Our lives were bought at a price, and consequently, they are no longer ours.

Just think about it. Jesus Christ paid the ultimate sacrifice with his life so that he could give back to us what was lost. God's only requirement is that we follow him in obedience so that we can walk with him, unhindered, in a life that's more abundant than one we could provide for ourselves on our own accord.

Are you ready to lay down your own plans and accept God's plan for your life? This is a very important decision. We all must stand before God one day and answer the question, "What did you do with my Son, Jesus Christ?"

There are two possible answers to that question. Only two.

"God, I accepted your Son, Jesus Christ, and your gift of salvation and have spent my life walking a journey of faith, guided by your word."

Or:

"God, I chose not to accept your provision as a way out of the penalties of my sin because I have not believed that Jesus Christ has paid them on my behalf. I chose instead, to live my life my own way."

There is no in-between. There are no excuses. Either you say "yes" to God's gift or "no." When you say, "yes," you are accepting life—an eternal place in God's family. When you say "No" or leave the question unanswered, you will suffer the consequences of sin as stated in Romans 6:23, which is death. Will you choose eternal death or eternal life? This is your choice today.

If you have never made the choice to receive the gift of salvation, now would be a perfect time. God's invitation is extended to you right now. All you need to do is pray the following prayer with a sincere heart.

Dear God, I confess that I am a sinner and I need your forgiveness. I accept the gift of salvation that you offer through your Son, Jesus Christ, today. As of this moment, I choose to live my life according to your plan for me and give up my own agenda because you love me and want the very best for my life. I can see that the way of this world only leads to eternal death, but your way, through the cross of Jesus Christ, leads me to life everlasting with you. That's what I choose—life with you. So, take my life and make me all yours. In Jesus' name, Amen.

If you just prayed this prayer today and have chosen to begin your walk with Christ, let me be the first to say, "Welcome to the family of God!"

Please take a moment to send me an email right now and let me know of this very important and life-changing decision. I would like to send you some materials so that you can learn more about your new life with Christ. This is just the beginning of an adventure of faith. The love of God has lifted you up, out of the old you and into the new you. It's a thrilling adventure with a great promise full of love, hope, joy and eternal life with our Father-God.

I look forward to meeting you, if not on this earth then in our eternal home in the Kingdom of Heaven with the entire Family of God. Let us hold fast to our eternal hope, for it is truly the evidence of God's gift of love to all who receive him.

Chapter Six:
God's Promises are Eternal

We fight best on our knees!

You've listened to my story and you've had an opportunity to respond to God's invitation to you. If you have already begun your walk of faith before reading this book, or if you recently accepted God's gift of salvation, the following section will be a source of strength for you.

In chapter four, I talked about switching my thinking from victim to soldier mentality. Remember I said that God's Word is powerful and effective in combating the battles in our mind and soul? It's true. Before continuing with this next section I suggest you read the book of Ephesians in the Bible. This chapter gives us the background for the whole idea of having a soldier mentality.

We've discussed how much God loves us and provided salvation for us so that we can live forever with him. He is the King of all Kings whose throne is in heaven. Once we are Christians, we inherit the citizenship of Heaven and our focus and direction in life reflects that change in status and identity. Or, at least, it should.

In a typical kingdom on earth, a royal family has certain privileges and benefits afforded them precisely because they bear the title or identity of the throne. Along with the position of honor and respect, they also have duties and obligations that must be taken seriously in order to rule well. It's not all glitz and glamour.

We as Christians have the privileges and benefits of being a Child of God; we read about those in God's Word.   However, we can't ignore the duties and obligations of the Christian life. We must "wear" our title with grace and dignity, yet we must remember challenges and difficulties are to be embraced as well. Just like in a natural earthly kingdom, along with the fanfare of royalty come life threats and enemy attack. Why do you think royal families have bodyguards and security personnel with them at all times? You can't expect to have the benefits without the risks. You could say it's a package deal.

If we stroll down the road of life wearing the title "Christian," we should be armed and ready for battle. Consider yourself a Warrior Princess or Warrior Prince, prepare yourself well, think thoughts that are in keeping with your title, and behave in such a manner that puts a proud smile on the face of your Father, the King.

Many times I've listened to the stories of other Christians and hear their sad discouragement. It becomes so obvious to me that they are listening to the lies of the enemy and NOT the truth of God's word. That is one reason I wrote this book. We, as Christian soldiers, must be prepared and not surprised by the enemy's tactics. When we lay our sword down in defeat, we're letting the enemy win, and there's no reason to do that.

I believe the main reason we shrink back from warfare is because we don't know *how* to fight. This section is designed to assist you in equipping and preparing yourself for certain spiritual warfare.

Look at Ephesians, chapter six. Paul is describing in detail the *"armor of God,"* teaching the Christian soldier how to suit up. I suggest that you begin each day "dressing" yourself with each piece of armor: The *helmet of salvation,* the *breastplate of righteousness,* the *belt of truth,* the *shield of faith,* the *sword of the spirit,* the *shoes of peace.* As you visualize clothing yourself with each piece of armor, you will strengthen your soul with the powerful truth of God's word. Every one of these elements of armor is yours as a soldier of God. You already possess them so you should wear them everywhere you go.

Take a good look in the mirror of God's word. Now, picture yourself a mighty warrior in God's army— trained and ready. Notice how Paul concludes the passage with verse 18, *"Do all this in prayer, asking for God's help. Pray on every occasion, as the Spirit leads... For this reason keep alert and never give up, pray always."*

The most effective warfare takes place when we are surrendered to God in our place of prayer, listening to his voice and holding on to his promises. We fight best on our knees, my fellow soldier. Never forget that we have at our disposal the most powerful weapon ever known to mankind—the *"Sword of the Spirit"*—known as the Bible.

The following prayers are almost word-for-word Scripture. The slight adaptations were made to make the prayer flow smoothly. Since we know that Scripture is God-given we know that these concepts and principles are more effective and powerful in prayer than any words we can conjure up on our own. As you fill in your own name to make it personal you are praying for the Word of God to come alive and active in your life. The more you pray prayers based on God's Word, the stronger you will be in your faith and the more victory you will see and experience in your every day life.

This is God's promise to you as his child. He intended for us to use these words as our mighty weapon to fight this fight of faith here on earth. Feel free to adapt these same prayers for your spouse, child, family member or friend.

Pray always

"This is the confidence we have in approaching God: that if we ask anything according to his will, he hears us." (1 John 5:14)

FOR GUIDANCE
Lord, I commit myself afresh to you. Thank you God, that you are continually with me and you hold me in your right hand. I pray you will guide me in your counsel all the days of my life. I pray that my delight and desire is in you and you alone. I will say, "My flesh and my heart may fail, but God is the rock and firm strength of my heart and my portion forever." Thank you for your guidance in my life to lead me in the best path, in Jesus name, I pray. Amen. (Psalm 73:23-26)

FOR PERSONAL KNOWLEDGE OF GOD
Lord, I pray that I would know you (have personal knowledge of you, be

acquainted with and understand you, appreciate, heed and cherish you) and serve you with a blameless heart and a willing mind. For you search the heart and mind and you understand all the wanderings of my thoughts. I pray that I would seek you (requiring you as my first and vital necessity), then I will be found by you. I ask that I will learn to place you in the center of my thoughts, mind and life more consistently, in Jesus name, Amen. (1 Chronicles 28:9)

FOR KEEPING GOD'S COMMANDS
Father, I pray that I will keep to your words and would lay up your commandments within my heart and treasure them. I pray that I would keep all of your commandments and that I would keep your law as the apple of my eye. I pray that your word would be the central focus in my life in all that I do and say. I ask that you would write your word on the tablet of my heart. May I say to Godly Wisdom, you are my sister and regard understanding and insight as an intimate friend, for then I will truly possess and walk in Godly wisdom for life, in Jesus' name. Amen. (Proverbs 7:1-4)

TO STAND FIRM IN SPIRITUAL WARFARE

Father, I pray that I will be strong in the Lord (be empowered through my union with you); I pray that I will draw strength from Christ (that strength which your boundless might provides). I pray that I will learn to put on YOUR whole armor (the armor of a heavy-armored soldier which God supplies), so that I may be able to successfully stand up against all the strategies and the deceits of the devil, in the mighty and victorious name of Jesus Christ, Amen. (Ephesians 6:10-11)

FOR JOY, PATIENCE & FAITHFULNESS

I pray that I may be joyful in hope, patient in affliction, and faithful in prayer. Thank you, Lord, that you protect me and defend me because I trust in you. May I acknowledge that it is you that gives me help and makes us glad; May I praise you with joyful songs. Lord, we know that weeping may endure for a night, but joy comes in the morning. Thank you for that. You have turned my sadness into a joyful dance; you have taken away (my) sorrow and surrounded me with joy. Amen. *(Romans 12:1, Psalm 28:7, 30:5)*

TO STRENGTHEN AND EQUIP

Lord, I pray that you will strengthen
(to complete and perfect) and make me
what I ought to be and equip me with
everything good so that I may carry out
your will, while you work in me and
accomplish that which is pleasing in your
sight, through Jesus Christ to whom
be the glory. And Lord I pray that we
will continue in the truths that we were
taught and firmly believe. I know who our
teachers were and remember that ever
since I was a child, and have known the
Holy Scriptures, which are able to give
wisdom that leads to salvation through
faith in Christ Jesus, Amen. (Hebrews
13:21, 2 Timothy 3:14, 15)

FOR ASSURANCE OF FAITH

Father, God, I thank you that I have
placed my trust in you, and shall be as
Mount Zion, which cannot be removed,
but abides for ever. Therefore being
justified by faith, I have peace with
You, Oh God through your son, Jesus
Christ. We know that we belong to you,
even though the whole world is under
the rule of the Evil one. We know that
the son of God has come and has given
us understanding, so that we may know
you, the true God. Thank you Lord,
that I live in union with you, the true
God and in union with your son Jesus

Christ. This is true, according to your word, God, and this is eternal life. I agree with your word and pray in Jesus name, Amen. (I John 5:19-20, Romans 5:1, Psalm 125:1)

TO BE ANXIETY FREE

Father, I ask in Jesus name that I would not fret or have any anxiety about anything, but in every circumstance and in everything, by prayer and petition (definite requests), with thanksgiving, continue to make my wants known to you. When we do that, you promise to grant to us peace (that tranquil state of soul peace), which transcends all understanding that shall mount guard over my heart and mind in Christ Jesus. I pray that the peace of Christ (of untroubled, undisturbed well-being) will be with me always. Amen. (Philippians 4:6-7)

FOR WALKING IN TRUTH & PEACE

I pray that I would stop worrying about even one thing, but in everything by prayer, whose essence is that of worship and devotion and by supplication, which is a cry for personal needs, and with thanksgiving, I'll let my requests for the things asked for be made known in the presence of God. And the peace of God, which surpasses all power of comprehension, shall mount guard over my heart and mind in Christ Jesus. May my mind be filled with those things that are good and that deserve praise; things that are true, noble, right, pure, lovely and honorable. May I put into practice what I learned and perceived from godly men and women, both by words and from actions. And I trust that according to your word, YOU who give us all peace will be with me. All this I ask according to your word. Amen. (Philippians 4:6-9)

FOR ABIDING IN CHRIST

Jesus, I ask that you would help me to daily dwell in you and you in me. May I live in you and you in me, abiding in (being vitally united to) you, as you are the vine. I pray that I would bear much (abundant) fruit as I abide in you and you in me. Remind me Lord, that apart from you, I can do nothing. I pray that I will choose to abide (vitally united with you, Jesus) and that your words would remain in me and continue to live in my heart, so that whatever I ask in your name, it will be done. I pray *my* life would bear (produce) much fruit and that the Father will be honored and glorified and that I would prove to be a true follower of Jesus Christ. Amen. (John 15:4-8)

FOR PEACE OF MIND

Jesus, you say to_____ (*your name*), "Peace I leave with you; my (own) peace I now give and bequeath to you. Not as the world gives do I give to you." Lord, I pray that I will heed your words and not allow my heart to be troubled, neither let it be afraid. Lord, I pray that I would stop allowing myself to be agitated and disturbed; and to not permit myself to be fearful or intimidated or cowardly and unsettled in this spirit. I pray your great peace over me especially when my temper is tried so that I can have a calm temper and enjoy a well-balanced mind, in Jesus name. Amen. (John 14:27)

TO BE SECURE IN CHRIST

Father, I pray that I would learn to be content (satisfied to the point where I'm not disturbed or disquieted) in whatever state I'm in. Help *me* to know how to live humbly in circumstances and also to know how to enjoy plenty and live in abundance. I pray that I would learn in any and all circumstances, the secret of facing every situation, whether well-fed or going hungry. I pray that I will have strength for all things in Christ who empowers me so that I may be sufficient in Christ's sufficiency. I pray that I would be an example of contentment to a watching world. Amen. (Philippians 4:11-13, I Timothy 6:6)

FOR GROWING IN FAITH

I thank you that I can be convinced and sure, that he who began a good work in me will continue until the day of Jesus Christ, developing (that good work) and perfecting and bringing it to full completion in me. Lord, I pray that you would continue to make me a man/ woman of God. I pray that I would flee from ungodly things, and that I would aim at and pursue righteousness (right standing with God and true goodness), godliness (which is the loving fear of God and being Christ like). I pray that I would grow in my faith, in love, in steadfastness (patience), and with gentleness of heart. Make me a man/woman after your own heart, in the mighty name of Jesus, Amen! (Philippians 1:6, 1 Timothy 6:11)

FOR REFUGE AND SHELTER

Father, I pray and ask that you would be merciful and gracious to me. May I take refuge and find shelter and confidence in you. Yes, I pray that I will take refuge in the shadow of your wings until the calamities and destructive storms pass. I pray that I would turn to you in the storm and cry out to the Most High who promises to perform on my behalf and will reward me (by bringing to pass your purposes for me) through this trial. I ask dear God that you would send forth your mercy and loving-kindness and I ask that your truth and your faithfulness would surround me at this time. Amen. (Psalm 57:1-3)

FOR VICTORY IN THE HARD TIMES

Lord, when I feel hedged in (pressed) on every side (troubled and oppressed in every way), I will not be cramped or crushed. I may suffer embarrassment and may be perplexed and unable to find a way out of this, but you promise not to drive me to despair. I may be pursued (persecuted and hard driven), but not deserted to stand alone. I may at times be struck down to the ground, but never struck out or destroyed. May I be assured that as you raised up our Lord Jesus, I too will be raised up and will be brought into your presence. I pray I would know that I am not alone and that you will carry me through the hard times. Amen. (2 Corinthians 4:8, 9, 14)

FOR DIVINE GUIDANCE

Lord, I ask that you would guide me continually and satisfy me in drought and in dry places and make me strong. I

ask that I would be like a watered garden
and like a spring of water whose waters
fail not. I pray that you would saturate
me with your Holy Spirit afresh today.
Thank you God, that you are continually
with me and you hold me in your right
hand. I pray that you will guide me with
your counsel all the days of my life. I
pray that my delight and desire is in you
and you alone. May I say, "my flesh and
my heart may fail, but God is the Rock
and firm strength of my heart and my
portion forever," in Jesus mighty name,
Amen. (Isaiah 58:11, Psalm 73:23-26)

FOR MY FUTURE AND HOPE

Father, I praise you for loving me and
desiring the best for me. Lord, eye has not
seen, ear has not heard or entered in the
heart of man all that you have prepared
(made and kept ready) for me as I love you
(as I affectionately, reverently, promptly
obey you) and gratefully recognize the
benefits you have bestowed upon me and
my life. Thank you, dear God, for your
goodness that you have laid up for me.
May I be planted and established in the
house of the Lord, may I flourish in the
courts of God. I pray I will continually
grow in grace, that I will still bring forth
fruit in old age. I ask that I would be full
of spiritual vitality and be rich in trust,
love and contentment. May my life be as

a living memorial to the faithfulness of God to show the watching world that the Lord is upright and faithful to all of his promises. In the name of Jesus, Amen. (1 Corinthians 2:9, Psalm 92:13-15)

This is my Bible

Here is a suggestion as you enter into a time of devotion and Bible study. Say this reading out loud and let the truth sink into your soul.

This is my Bible
I believe the words in this book are true
It is the Holy, infallible word of God
I believe God is who it says He is
I believe that He will do what it says he will do
This is the light for my path ahead
This is food for my soul
It is alive and powerful
It is my weapon against the enemy, Satan
I believe that I am who it says I am
I can do what it says I can do
I am a precious child of God
I am more than a conqueror
I am the righteousness of God in Christ Jesus
And I walk by faith and not by sight
As God gives me strength
I will live my life in obedience to his word
This is my Bible

The Word about Widows

The first year I was widowed I desperately searched the Scriptures from Genesis to Revelation and wrote down every verse that mentioned widows. I was so eager to hear what God had to say about those of us who had lost our husbands through death. It was so uplifting for me to read over and over again that God highly esteems the widow and protects her with a very special covering—a divine covering that is impenetrable. I've highlighted the word *widow* in each verse for emphasis.

> *Do not take advantage of a **widow** or an orphan. If you do and they cry out to me, I will certainly hear their cry. My anger will be aroused, and I will kill you with a sword; your wives will become **widows** and your children fatherless.* (Exodus 22:22-24)

> *For the Lord your God is God of gods and Lord of Lords, the great God, mighty and awesome, who shows no partiality and accepts no bribes. He defends the*

*cause of the fatherless and the **widow**, and loves the alien, giving him food and clothing.* (Deuteronomy 10:17-18)

*At the end of every three years, bring all the tithes of that year's produce and store it in your towns, so that the Levites (who have no allotment or inheritance of their own) and the aliens, the fatherless and the **widows** who live in your towns may come and eat and be satisfied, and so that the Lord your God may bless you in all the work of your hands.* (Deuteronomy 14:28-29)

*Do not deprive the alien or the fatherless of justice, or take the cloak of the **widow** as a pledge. Remember that you were slaves in Egypt and the Lord your God redeemed you from there. That is why I command you to do this. When you are harvesting in your field and you overlook a sheaf, do not go back to get it. Leave it for the alien, the fatherless and the **widow**, so that the Lord your God may bless you in all the work of your hands. When you beat the olives from your trees, do not go over the branches a second time. Leave what remains for the alien, the fatherless and the **widow**. When you harvest the grapes in your vineyard, do not go over the vines again. Leave what remains for the alien, the fatherless and the **widow**. Remember that you were slaves* *in Egypt. That is why I command you to do this.* (Deuteronomy 24:17-22)

*If brothers are living together and one of them dies without a son, his **widow** must not marry outside the family. Her husband's brother shall take her and marry her and fulfill the duty of a brother-in-law to her. The first son she bears shall carry on the name of the dead brother so that his name will not be blotted out from Israel.* (Deuteronomy 25:5-6)

*Cursed is the man who withholds justice from the alien, the fatherless or the **widow**.* (Deuteronomy 27:19)

*Is not your wickedness great? Are not your sins endless? .... And you sent **widows** away empty-handed and broke the strength of the fatherless.* (Job 22:5, 9)

*Why does the Almighty not set times for judgment? ...They drive away the orphan's donkey and take the **widow's** ox in pledge... They prey on the barren and the childless woman, and to the **widow** show no kindness. But God drags away the mighty by his power; though they become established, they have no assurance of life. He may let them rest in a feeling of security, but his eyes are on their ways.* (Job 24:21-23)

*Whoever heard me spoke well of me,
and those who saw me commended me,
because I rescued the poor who cried for
help, and the fatherless who had none
to assist him. The man who was dying
bless me; I made the* **widow's** *heart sing.*
(Job 29:13)

*If I have denied the desire of the poor or
let the eyes of the* **widow** *grow weary,
if I have kept my bread to myself, not
sharing it with the fatherless – but from
my youth I reared him as would a father,
and from my birth I guided the* **widow**.
(Job 31:16-18)

*A father to the fatherless, a defender
of* **widows**, *is God in his holy dwelling.*
(Psalm 68:5)

*Lord, the God who avenges, shine forth...
they crush your people, O Lord... they slay
the* **widow** *and the alien; they murder
the fatherless.* (Psalm 94:1, 5, 6)

*Blessed is he whose help is the God of
Jacob, whose hope is in the Lord his
God, the Maker of heaven and earth...
He upholds the cause of the oppressed
and gives food to the hungry. The Lord
sets prisoners free, the Lord gives sight
to the blind, the Lord lifts up those who
are bowed down, the Lord loves the*

*righteous. The Lord watches over the alien and sustains the fatherless and the **widow**, but he frustrates the ways of the wicked.* (Psalm 146:5-9)

*The Lord tears down the proud man's house but he keeps the **widow's** boundaries intact.* (Proverbs 15:25)

*When you spread out your hands in prayer, I will hide my eyes from you; even if you offer many prayers, I will not listen. Your hands are full of blood; wash and make yourselves clean. Take your evil deeds out of my sight! Stop doing wrong, learn to do right! Seek justice, encourage the oppressed. Defend the cause of the fatherless, plead the case of the **widow**.* (Isaiah 1:15-17)

*Woe to those who make unjust laws, to those who issue oppressive decrees, to deprive the poor of their rights and rob my oppressed people of justice, making **widows** their prey and robbing the fatherless.* (Isaiah 10:1, 2)

Hear the word of the Lord... reform your ways and your actions and I will let you live in this place. Do not trust in deceptive words and say, "This is the temple of the Lord," ...If you really change your ways and your actions and deal with each *other justly, if you do not oppress the alien, the fatherless or the **widow** and do not shed innocent blood in this place, and if you do not follow other gods to your own harm, then I will let you live in this place...* (Jeremiah 7:2-7)

*This is what the Lord says: Do what is just and right. Rescue from the hand of his oppressor the one who has been robbed. Do no wrong or violence to the alien, the fatherless or the **widow**, and do not shed innocent blood in this place.* (Jeremiah 22:3)

*Leave your orphans; I will protect their lives. Your **widows** too can trust in me.* (Jeremiah 49:11)

*This is what the Lord Almighty says: 'Administer true justice; show mercy and compassion to one another. Do not oppress the **widow** or the fatherless, the alien or the poor. In our hearts do not think evil of each other.'* (Zechariah 7:9, 10)

*"So I will come near to you for judgment. I will be quick to testify against sorcerers, adulterers and perjurers, against those who defraud laborers of their wages, who oppress the **widows** and the fatherless, and deprive aliens of justice, but do not fear me." Says the Lord Almighty.* (Malachi 3:5)

Woe to you, teachers of the law and Pharisees, you hypocrites! You devour **widows'** *houses and for show make lengthy prayers.   Therefore you will be punished more severely.* (Matthew 23:14, Mark 12:40, Luke 20:47)

In those days when the number of disciples was increasing, the Grecian Jews among them complained against those of the Aramaic-speaking community because their **widows** *were being overlooked in the daily distribution of food.* (Acts 6:1)

Give proper recognition to those **widows** *who are really in need. But if a* **widow** *has children or grandchildren, these should learn first of all to put their religion into practice by caring for their own family and so repaying their parents and grandparents, for this is pleasing to God. The* **widow** *who is really in need and left alone puts her hope in God and continues night and day to pray and to ask God for help.* (1 Timothy 5:3-5)

As for younger **widows**, *do not put them on such a list. For when their sensual desires overcome their dedication to Christ, they want to marry... so I counsel younger widows to marry, to have children, to manage their homes and to give the enemy no opportunity for slander. If any woman who is a believer has* *__widows__ in her family, she should help them and not let the church be burdened with them, so that the church can help those __widows__ who are really in need.* (1 Timothy 5:11-16)

If anyone considers himself religious and yet does not keep a tight rein on his tongue, he deceives himself and his religion is worthless. Religion that God our Father accepts as pure and faultless is this: to look after orphans and __widows__ in their distress and to keep oneself from being polluted by the world. (James 1:26, 27)

Finally, I leave you with these inspiring words from Joshua, a great Hebrew warrior: "*...Be strong and of good courage; do not be afraid, nor be dismayed, for the Lord your God is with you wherever you go.*" (Joshua 1:9) NKJV

Endnotes

Prayers in chapter six created from *New King James Version (NKJV)*, *New International Version (NIV)*, *Today's New International Version (TNIV)* and the *Amplified Version*. Other Scriptures throughout the book are taken from the *New International Version (NIV)*, unless otherwise noted. International Bible Society. Zondervan Bible Publishers. With permission.

1. Excerpts from the Hymn *The Solid Rock*. (William B. Bradbury/Edward Mote) Third Verse. Public domain.

2. Taken from *For Those Who Hurt* by Charles R. Swindoll. Copyright 1960, 1962, 1963, 1968, 1971, 1972, 1973, 1975 by The Lockman Foundation, New American Standard Bible. Used by permission of Zondervan.

3. Smith, Hannah Whitall. *The Christian's Secret of a Happy Life*. (Grand Rapids, MI: Fleming H. Revell Company) Page 78. Public domain.

Printed in the United States
87289LV00002B/103-198/A